John Coleman

THE
TAVISTOCK INSTITUTE
FOR HUMAN RELATIONS

Shaping the Moral, Spiritual, Cultural,
Political and Economic Decline
of the United States.

OMNIA VERITAS.

John Coleman

John Coleman is a British author and former member of the Secret Intelligence Service. Coleman has produced various analyses of the Club of Rome, the Giorgio Cini Foundation, Forbes Global 2000, the Interreligious Peace Colloquium, the Tavistock Institute, the Black Nobility and other organisations with New World Order themes.

The Tavistock Institute of Human Relations
Shaping the Moral, Spiritual, Cultural,
Political, and Economic Decline
of the United States of America

Published par Omnia Veritas Limited

© Omnia Veritas Ltd – 2024
⊘MNIA VERITAS®
www.omnia-veritas.com

The Tavistock Institute for Human Relations has had a profound effect on the moral, spiritual, cultural, political and economic policies of the United States of America and Great Britain. It has been in the front line of the attack on the U.S. Constitution and State constitutions. No group did more to propagandize the U.S. to participate in the WWI at a time when the majority of the American people were opposed to it.

Much the same tactics were used by the Social Science scientists at Tavistock to get the United States into WWII, Korea, Vietnam, Serbia and both wars against Iraq. Tavistock began as a propaganda creating and disseminating organization at Wellington House in London in the run-up to WWI, what Toynbee called "that black hole of disinformation." On another occasion Toynbee called Wellington House "a lie factory." From a somewhat crude beginning, Wellington House evolved into the Tavistock Institute and went on to shape the destiny of Germany, Russia, Britain and the United States in a highly controversial manner. The people of these nations were unaware that they were being "brainwashed." The origin of "mind control," "inner directional conditioning" and mass "brainwashing" is explained in an easy to understand book written with great authority.

The fall of dynasties, the Bolshevik Revolution, WWI and WWII saw the destruction of old alliances and boundaries, the convulsions in religion, morals, family life, economic and political conduct, decadence in music and art can all be traced back to mass indoctrination (mass brainwashing) practiced by the Tavistock Institute Social Science scientists. Prominent among Tavistock's faculty were Edward Bernays, the double nephew of Sigmund Freud. It is said that Herr Goebbels, Propaganda Minister in the German Third Reich used methodology devised by Bernays as well as those of Willy Munzenberg, whose extraordinary career is touched upon in this work about the past, present and future. Without Tavistock, there would have been no WWI and WWII, no Bolshevik Revolution, Korea, Vietnam, Serbia and Iraq wars. But for Tavistock, the United States would not be rushing down the road to dissolution and collapse.

Acknowledgements

My very great debt - an immense one - for the help, encouragement and hard and long hours, sound criticism and encouragement on this book that my wife Lena, and our son John provided at every stage of its preparation, including suggestions for the cover design, research and proof reading.

I also owe a debt of gratitude to Dana Farnes for his untiring computer work and technical assistance; to Ann Louise Gittleman, and James Templeton, who encouraged me to write this book and gave me no peace until I began it; to Renee and Grant Magan for doing the daily work, leaving me free to concentrate on writing. My particular thanks also to Dr. Kinne McCabe and Mike Granston whose faithful and steadfast support was a key factor in enabling me to finish the work.

FOREWORD

The Tavistock Institute of Human Relations was unknown to the people of the United States before Dr. Coleman exposed its existence in his monograph, The Tavistock Institute of Human Relations: Britain's Control of the United States. Up to that time, Tavistock had successfully retained its secretive role in shaping the affairs of the United States, its government and its people since its early beginning in London, in 1913 at Wellington House.

Since Dr. Coleman's original article exposing this ultra- secret organization, others have come forward with claims of authorship, which they were unable to substantiate.

Tavistock began as a propaganda creating and disseminating organization centered at Wellington House, which was where the original organization was put together with intent of shaping a propaganda outlet that would break down the stiff public resistance being encountered to the looming war between Britain and Germany.

The project was given to Lords Rothmere and Northcliffe and their mandate was to produce an organization capable of manipulating public opinion and directing that manufactured opinion down the desired pathway to support for a declaration of war by Great Britain against Germany.

Funding was provided by the British royal family, and later by the Rothschilds to whom Lord Northcliffe was related through marriage. Arnold Toynbee was selected as Director of Future Studies. Two Americans, Walter Lippmann and Edward Bernays were appointed to handle the manipulation of American public opinion in preparation for the entry of the United States into WWI, and to brief and direct President Woodrow Wilson.

From a somewhat crude beginning at Wellington House, grew an organization that was to shape the destiny of Germany, Britain and more especially the United States in manner that became a highly sophisticated organization to manipulate and create public opinion, what is commonly termed, "mass brainwashing."

During the course of its evolvement, Tavistock expanded in size and ambition, when in 1937, a decision was made to use the German author Oswald Spengler's monumental work, *Untergange des Abenlandes* (The Decline of Western Civilization) as a model.

Previously, Wellington House board members Rothmere, Northcliffe, Lippmann, and Bernays had read and proposed as a guide the writings of Correa Moylan Walsh, in particular, the book The Climax of Civilization (1917) as corresponding closely to conditions that had to be created before a New World Order in a One World Government could be ushered in.

In this endeavor the members of the board consulted with the British royal family and obtained the approval of the "Olympians" (the inner core of the Committee of 300) to formulate a strategy. Funding was provided by the monarchy, the Rothschilds, the Milner Group and the Rockefeller family trusts.

In 1936, Spengler's monumental work had come to the attention of what had become the Tavistock Institute. In preparation for changing and reshaping public opinion for the second time in less than twelve years, by unanimous consent of the board, Spengler's massive book was adopted as the blueprint for a new working model to bring about the decline and fall of Western civilization necessary to create and establish a New World Order inside a One World Government.

Spengler held it bound to happen that alien elements would be introduced into Western civilization in increasing numbers, and that the West would fail at that time to expel the aliens, thereby sealing its fate, a society, whose inward beliefs and sound convictions would become at variance with its outward profession and thus Western civilization would fall by the wayside in the manner of the ancient civilizations of Greece and Rome.

Tavistock thinking was that Spengler had indoctrinated Western civilization to believe that it would err on the side of Roman civilization, and expel the aliens. The genetic loss that has fallen upon Europe-and especially on Scandinavia, England, Germany, France-(the Anglo-Saxon, Nordic Alpine Germanic races) that began just before the Second World War is already so great as to be beyond expectations, and continues at an alarming pace under the skilled guidance of the Tavistock managers.

What was a very rare instance became a common occurrence, a black man married to a white women or vice-versa.

The two World Wars cost the German nation almost one quarter of its population. Most of the intellectual energies of the German nation were diverted into war channels in defense of the Fatherland at the expense of science, arts, literature, music and the cultural, spiritual and moral advancement of the nation. The same could be said of the British nation. The blaze kindled by the British under the direction of Tavistock set all of Europe on fire, and did incalculable damage according to the Tavistock blueprint that matched Spengler's predictions.

Classical and Western are the only two civilizations that could bring a modern renaissance to the world. They had flourished and progressed just as long as these civilizations remained under the control of the Anglo-Saxon Nordic Alpine, Germanic races. The unsurpassed beauty of their literature, art, their classics, spiritual and moral advancement of the female sex with a very large corresponding degree of protection, was what distinguished Western and Classic civilizations from others.

It was this bastion that Spengler saw coming under increasing attack and the thinking at Tavistock ran on parallel tracks, but with a totally different goal. Tavistock saw this civilizations a stumbling block to ushering a New World Order, as did the emphasis on protection and elevation of the female sex to a place of high respect and honor.

Thus the whole thrust of Tavistock was to "democratize" the West by an attack on womanhood, and the racial, moral, spiritual and religious foundation upon which Western civilization rested.

As Spengler suggested, the Greeks and Romans were devoted to the social, religious, moral and spiritual advancement and the preservation of womanhood and they were successful for just as long as they were in control and could arrange matters so that government was carried out by a limited number of responsible citizens supported by the general populace below them, all being of the same pure unadulterated race. The planners at Tavistock saw that the way to upset the balance of Western civilization was to force unwelcome changes in the race by removing control from the deserving to the undeserving in the manner of ancient Roman leaders who were supplanted by their former slaves and aliens, whom they had permitted to come and dwell among them.

Tavistock, by 1937, had come a long way from its Wellington House beginnings and the successful propaganda campaign that had turned the British public from being strongly anti-war in 1913 to willing participants through the arts of manipulation with the willing cooperation of news communications media.

The technique was carried across the Atlantic in 1916 to manipulate the American people to support of the war in Europe. In spite of the fact that the vast majority, including at least 50 U.S. Senators were adamantly opposed to the U.S. getting dragged into what they perceived was essentially a quarrel between Britain and France on the one hand, and Germany on the other, largely over trade and economics, the conspirators were undeterred. At that point Wellington House introduced the word, "Isolationists" as a derogatory description of those Americans who opposed U.S. participation in the war. The use of such words and phrases has proliferated under the expert brainwashing of the Social sciences scientists at Tavistock. Terms like "regime change," "collateral damage" became almost new English language.

With the Tavistock plan modified to suit American conditions, Bernays and Lippmann led President Woodrow Wilson to set up the very first Tavistock methodology techniques for polling (manufacturing) so-called public opinion created by Tavistock propaganda. They also taught Wilson to set up a secret body of "managers" to run the war effort and a body of "advisors" to assist the President in his decision-making. The Creel Commission was the first such body of opinion-makers set up in the United States.

Woodrow Wilson was the first American president to publicly proclaim himself in favor of a Socialist New World Order inside a Socialist One World Government. His remarkable acceptance of the New World Order is found in his book *The New Freedom*.

We say "his" book, but actually, it was written by Socialist William B. Hayle. Wilson denounced capitalism. "It is contrary to the common man and it has brought stagnation to our economy," Wilson wrote.

Yet, at the time, the United States economy was enjoying prosperity and industrial expansion as it had never experienced before in its history:

"We stand in the presence of a revolution—not a bloody revolution, America is not given to spilling blood—but a silent revolution, whereby America will insist upon recovering to practice those ideals which she has always professed, upon securing a government devoted to the general and not the special interests. We are upon the threshold of a time when the systematic life of the country will be sustained or at least supplemented at every point by government activity. And now we have to determine what kind of a government activity it shall be; whether, in the first place, it shall be directed from government itself, or whether it shall be indirect, through instrumentalities which have already constituted themselves and which stand ready to supersede government."

While the U.S. was still a neutral power under the Wilson presidency, Wellington House poured out a cadence of lies about Germany, and what a threat it was to America.

We are reminded of the statement made by Bakunin in 1814 as it tied in so well with the outrageous propaganda that Wilson made use of to bolster his case:

"Lying by diplomacy: Diplomacy has no other mission. Every time a State wants to declare war upon another State, it starts off by launching a manifesto addressed not only to its own subjects but also to the whole world. In this manifesto it declares that right and justice are on its side and endeavors to prove that it is actuated by love of peace and humanity (and democracy), and that, imbued with generous and peaceful sentiments, it suffered for a long time in silence until mounting iniquity of its enemy forced it to bare its sword."

"At the same time it vows that, disdainful of all material conquest and not seeking any increase in territory, it will put an end to this war as soon as justice is reestablished. And its antagonist's answer with a similar manifesto, in which, naturally, right, justice and humanity and all generous sentiments are to be found respectively on its side. These mutually opposed manifestos are written with the same eloquence, they breath the same righteous indignation, and one is just as sincere as the other, that is to say they are both brazen in their lies, and it is only fools who are deceived by them. Sensible persons, all those who have some political experience do not even take the trouble of reading such manifestos."

President Wilson's statements just before he went to the Congress to request a constitutional declaration of war embodies every one of Bakunin's sentiments.

He was "lying by diplomacy" and he used the gross propaganda manufactured at Wellington House to inflame the American public by tales of atrocities committed by the German Army in its march across Belgium in 1914. As we shall discover, it was, for the most part, a gigantic lie passed off as truth.

I remember looking through a large stack of old newspapers at the British Museum where I spent five years doing in- depth research. The papers covered the years 1912 to 1920. I recall thinking at the time: "Isn't it amazing that the rush to the New World Order Socialist totalitarian government should be led by the United States, supposedly a bastion of freedom?"

Then, as I recall, it came to me with great clarity that the Committee of 300 has its people at the highest and lowest echelons embedded in the U.S., in banking, industry, trade, defense, the State Department and indeed in the very White House, not to mention the Elite Club called the U.S. Senate, which in my view is a forum for pushing the New World Order."

I recall thinking that President Wilson's propaganda blast against Germany and the Kaiser (actually the product of Rothschild agents Lords Northcliffe and Rothmere, and the Wellington House propaganda factory) was not much different to the "contrived situation" of Pearl Harbor, the Gulf of Tonkin "incident" and looking back now I can see no difference between the propaganda lies about the brutality of German soldiers allegedly chopping off the arms and legs of little Belgian children in 1914, than the methods used to get the American people duped and doped into allowing the Bush administration to invade Iraq. Whereas in 1914 it was the Kaiser who was a "brute savage," a "ruthless murderer", a "monster", the "Butcher of Berlin", in 2002 it was President Hussein who was all of these things and a whole lot more, including the "Butcher of Baghdad!" Poor duped, deluded, deceived, connived, trustful, America! When will you ever learn?

In 1917 the New World Order agenda was being rushed through the House and Senate by Woodrow Wilson, and President Bush forced the New World Order agenda for Iraq through the House and Senate in 2002 without debate, an exercise in arbitrary power and a gross violation of the U.S. Constitution for which the American people are paying a huge price. But the American people are suffering from toxic shock induced by the Tavistock Institute of Human Relations and the American people are in a state of sleepwalking and without leadership.

They do not know what the price is and do not care to find out. The Committee of 300 continues to rule the United States, just as it did in the Wilson and Roosevelt presidencies, while the American people were distracted with "bread and circuses" only today it is baseball, football, endless Hollywood, and Social Security. Nothing has changed.

The United States, harried, hounded, pushed and shoved is headed of a fast track to the New World Order, propelled along by the Radical Republicans of the War Party who have been taken over by the scientists at the Tavistock Institute for Human Relations.

Just recently I was asked by a subscriber "where do we find the Tavistock Institute?" My response was: "Look around the U.S. Senate, the House of Representatives, the White House, the State Department, the Defense Department, Wall Street, Fox T.V. (Faux T.V.) and you will see their change agents in every one of these places."

President Wilson was the first U.S. president to "manage" the war through a civilian committee guided and directed by the Bernays and Lippmann from Wellington House, to which we have already made mention.

The resounding success of Wellington House and its enormous influence on the course of American history began before that in 1913. Wilson had spent almost a year tearing down the protective trade tariffs that had defended the American domestic markets from being overwhelmed by "Free Trade," essentially the practice of allowing cheap British goods made with cheap labor in India to flood the American market. On October 12, 1913 Wilson signed the bill that was the beginning of the end of the unique American middle class, long the target of the Fabian Socialists. The bill was described as a measure to "adjust tariffs," but it would have been accurate to describe it as a bill to "destroy tariffs."

Such was the hidden power of Wellington House that the vast majority of the American people accepted this lie, not knowing or realizing that it was a death knell for American commerce that would lead to NAFTA, GATT and the World Trade Organization (WTO). Even more astonishing was the acceptance of the Federal Income Tax Act that was passed on September 5, 1913, to replace trade tariffs as the source of revenue for the Federal Government. Income Tax is a Marxist doctrine not found in the U.S. Constitution anymore than the Federal Reserve Bank is found in the Constitution. Wilson called his twin blows against the Constitution, "a fight for the people, and for free business," and said he was proud to have taken "part in the completion of a great piece of business..." The Federal Reserve Act, explained by Wilson as "reconstructing the Nation's banking and currency system" was rushed through on a flood-tide of propaganda emanating from Wellington House, just in time for the hostilities that began the horror of WWI.

Most historians are agreed that without passage of the Federal Reserve Bank Act, Lord Grey would not have been able to start that terrible conflagration.

The deceptive language of the Federal Reserve Act was under the guidance of Bernays and Lippman who set up a "National Citizen's League" with the notorious Samuel Untermeyer as its chairman, to promote the Federal Reserve Bank, that secured control of the people's money and currency and transferred it to a private monopoly without the victim's consent.

One of the most interesting pieces of history surrounding the imposition of the foreign financial slavery measure was that before it was sent to Wilson for his signature, a copy was given to the sinister Colonel Edward Mandel House as the representative of Wellington House and the British oligarchy represented by the banker, J.P. Morgan.

As to the American people, in whose name the disastrous measure was instituted, they had not the faintest idea how they had been connived, cheated, lied to and utterly deceived. An instrument of slavery was fastened around their necks without the victims ever becoming aware of it.

Wellington House methodology was at its height when Wilson was coached in how to persuade Congress to declare war on Germany, although he had won election on the solemn promise to keep America out of the war then raging in Europe, a great triumph for the new art of public opinion making. It was just that - the poll questions were shaded in such away that the answers reflected the opinions of the public; not their understanding of the questions, nor their understanding of the processes of political science.

A thorough search and reading of the Congressional Records from 1910 to 1920 by this writer showed very clearly that had Wilson not signed the iniquitous "currency reform" bill on December 23, 1913, the upper-level parallel secret government of the United States foretold by H.G. Wells would not have been able to commit the vast resources of the United States to the war in Europe.

The House of Morgan representing the "Olympians" of the Committee of 300, and its all powerful City of London financial nexus, played a leading role in shaping the "U.S. Federal Reserve Banks," which were neither "Federal" nor "banks," but a private money-generating monopoly fastened around the necks of the American people whose money was now free to be stolen on an unimaginable scale, making them slaves of the New World Order inside the coming One World Government. The Great Depression of the 1930s was the second major catastrophic bill the American people had to pay, the first being World War I. (See Appendix)

Those who read this book as a first introduction to the New World Order inside a One World Government will be skeptical; but consider that no less a personage than the great Sir Harold Mackinder did not hide his beliefs about its coming.

More than that, he gave notice that it might be a dictatorship. Sir Harold had an impressive resume (CV) having been Professor of Geography at the University of London; a director of the London School of Economics from 1903-1908 and a Member of Parliament from 1910-1922. He was also a close associate of Arnold Toynbee one of the leading lights at Wellington House. He had correctly predicted a core of startling geopolitical events, many of them actually coming to pass.

One such "prophecy" was the founding of two Germanys, the Social Democratic Republic of Germany and the Federal Republic of Germany. Critics suggested that he got the information from Toynbee; that it was merely the long range planning of the Committee of 300 that Toynbee knew about.

After Wellington House, Toynbee moved to the Royal Institute for International Affairs (RIIA), and then to London University where he held the chair for International History. In his book, America and World Revolution he said:

"If we are to avoid mass-suicide, we must have our world- state quickly and this probably means that we must have it in a non-democratic form to begin with. We will have to start building a world-state now on the best design that is practicable at the moment."

Toynbee went on in a forthright manner saying this "world dictatorship" would have to supplant "the local national states which litter the present political map."

The new world-state was to be brought about on the basis of mass mind control and propaganda that would make it acceptable. I explained in my book The Committee of 300, that Bernays "blew the whistle" on polling in his 1923 and 1928 books, Propaganda, and Crystallizing Public Opinion.

This was followed by Engineering Consent:

Self-preservation, ambition, pride, hunger, love of family and children, patriotism, imitativeness, the desire to be a leader, love of play-these and other drives are the psychological raw materials which every leader must take into account in his endeavor to win the public to his point of view... To maintain their self-assurance, most people need to feel certain that whatever they believe about anything is true.

These revealing works are examined and we should add that in writing them, the Tavistock hierarchy apparently felt secure enough to gloat over their control of the United States and Great Britain that had blossomed into an open conspiracy along the lines first suggested by H.G. Wells.

With the advent of Wellington House, funded by the British monarchy and later by Rockefeller, Rothschild and the United

States, Western civilization entered into the first phase of a plan that would provide a secret government to rule the world, namely, the Committee of 300.

Tavistock Institute of Human Relations was its creation. As this book is not about the Committee of 300, we would suggest that readers obtain copies of the first and second book, The Committee of 300.

The "300's" carefully structured blueprint has been followed to the letter and today as we reach the end of 2005, looking back it is fairly easy for knowledgeable persons to trace the course that was laid out for Western civilization and to mark its progression to the point where we are today. This book is an attempt to do just that.

CHAPTER 1

Founding the World's Premiere Brainwashing Institute

From its modest but vitally important beginning at Wellington House, the Tavistock Institute for Human Relations expanded rapidly to become the world's premier top-secret "brainwashing" institute." How this rapid progression was accomplished needs to be explained.

The modern science of mass manipulation of public opinion was born at Wellington House, London, the lusty infant being midwifed by Lord Northcliffe and Lord Rothmere.

The British monarchy, Lord Rothschild, and the Rockefellers were responsible for funding the venture. The papers we were privileged to examine showed that the purpose of those at Wellington House was to effect a change in the opinion of the British people who were adamantly opposed to war with Germany, a formidable task that was accomplished by "opinion making" through polling. The staff consisted of Arnold Toynbee, a future director of studies at the Royal Institute of International Affairs (RIIA), Lords Northcliffe, and the Americans, Walter Lippmann and Edward Bernays.

Bernays was born in Vienna on November 22, 1891. As the nephew of Sigmund Freud the father of psychoanalysis, regarded by many as "the father of public relations" although the title properly belongs to Willy Munzenberg. Bernays pioneered the use of psychology and other social sciences to shape and form public opinion so that the public thought such manufactured opinions were their own.

"If we understand the mechanism and motives of the group mind, it is now possible to control and regiment the masses according to our will without them knowing it." Bernays postulated. He called this technique "Engineering Consent. One of his best-known techniques of achieving this goal was the indirect use of what he called third party authorities to shape the desired opinions: "If you can influence the leaders, either with or without their conscious cooperation, you automatically influence the group which they sway. This technique he called "opinion making."

Perhaps we can now begin to understand how it was that Wilson, Roosevelt, Clinton, Bush the elder and the younger could so easily lead American into disastrous wars in which its people should never have become involved.

The joint British and American participants concentrated their efforts on techniques as yet not tried out, to mobilize support for the war looming on the horizon.

As previously stated, the British people did not want war, and said so, but Toynbee, Lippmann and Bernays expected to change that by applying techniques designed to manipulate public opinion through the use of polling. Herein we provide a review of the methods that were devised and executed to bring Great Britain and the United States into the First World War, plus the techniques that were put into practice between the two World Wars and beyond. As will be seen propaganda was to play a major role.

One of the main objectives at Tavistock was to achieve the degradation of women. Tavistock recognized that Jesus Christ has brought a new place of respect in the order of civilization to womanhood, which prior to his coming had not been present.

After Christ's ministry, womanhood gained a respect and a high place in society absent from pre-Christian civilizations. Of course it can be argued that such an elevated status existed in the Greek and Roman empires, and that would be true to a certain extent, but not to the extent that womanhood was elevated in post-Christ society.

Tavistock sought to change that and the process began immediately after WWI. The Eastern Orthodox Church which the Rus (Viking) princes of Moscow brought back from Constantinople, revered and respected womanhood, and their experience with the Khazarians whom they subsequently defeated and drove out of Russia, left them determined to protect womanhood in Russia.

The founder of the Romanov dynasty, Michael Romanov was the scion of a noble family that had defended Russia on the basis of a Christian country. From 1613 the Romanovs sought to ennoble Russia and imbue it with a great spirit of Christianity, which meant also, protection for and the honoring of Russian womanhood.

The Princes of Moscow under Prince Dimitri Donskoi earned the unremitting hatred of the Rothschilds for Russia because of Donskoi's defeat and expulsion of the Khazarian hordes that inhabited the lower-regions of the Volga. This barbaric warrior nation of mysterious Indo-Turk origin, had adopted the Judaic religion on passage of a decree by King Bulant after the religion was approved by the chief Khazarian soothsayer-magician-sorcerer, David el-Roi.

It was el Roi's personal flag, now called the "Star of David" that became the official flag of the Khazarian nation when they settled in Poland after being forced out of Russia.

The flag was adopted by the Zionists as their standard and is still mistakenly called the "Star of David." Christians make the error of confusion linking it with the Old Testament King David, when in fact there is no relation between the two.

The hatred of Russia was compounded in 1612 when the Romanov dynasty led a Russian Army against Poland taking back large parts of Poland that had formerly belonged to Russia.

The principal architect of enmity brought to bear against Russia was the Rothschild dynasty and it was this burning hatred that Tavistock used and channeled in its plan to destroy Western civilization.

The first opportunity created by Tavistock came in 1905 with the attack by the Japanese Navy that completely surprised the Russian Fleet. The exercise was bankrolled by Jacob Schiff, the Wall Street banker, who was related to Rothschild.

The defeat of the Russian fleet at Port Arthur in a surprise attack marked the beginning of the pall of gloom that was about to roll in over Christian Europe. The Rockefeller Standard Oil Group directed by Tavistock and with the aid of the "300" engineered the Russo-Japanese War. The money used to finance the operation came from Jacob Schiff, but was actually provided by the Rockefeller General Education Board, whose outward purpose was to finance Negro education. All of the propaganda and advertising for the board was written and crafted by the Social scientists at Tavistock, which was then called "Wellington House."

In 1941 another Rockefeller front organization, the Institute for Pacific Relations (IPR) gave large sums to its Japanese counterpart in Tokyo. The money was then funneled to a member of the imperial family by Richard Sorge, a Russian master-spy, for the purposes of inducing Japan to attack the United States at Pearl Harbor. Again, Tavistock was the originator of all of IPR's publications.

Although it was not yet evident, as Spengler was to mention in his monumental work, published in 1936, it marked the beginning of the end of the old order. Contrary to most establishment accounts of history, the "Russian" revolution was not a Russian revolution at all, but a foreign ideology backed primarily by the Committee of 300 and its arm, the Tavistock Institute, that was violently forced upon a startled, unprepared and dismayed Romanov family.

It was political warfare, low grade warfare and psychological warfare in which Tavistock had become well versed.

As Winston Churchill was to remark: "They transported Lenin in a sealed truck like a plague bacillus from Switzerland into Russia," and then once established "Lenin and Trotsky seized Russia by the hair of its head."

Much has been written (but nearly always in passing as if it is a mere postscript to history) about the "sealed truck," "sealed car," "sealed train," that transported Lenin and his Bolshevik revolutionaries safely through the midst of war-torn Europe and deposited them in Russia, there to begin their imported Bolshevik Revolution so mistakenly termed the "Russian Revolution."

Documents the author was privileged to study at Wellington House and what was revealed in the Arnold Toynbee papers and Bruce Lockhart's private papers, led to the conclusion that without Toynbee, Bruce Lockhart of MI6 British intelligence and without the complicity of at least five European nations, ostensibly loyal and friendly with the Court at St. Petersburg, the merciless Bolshevik Revolution would have been still-born.

As this account must of necessity be limited to Tavistock's participation in the affair, it will not be as a complete account of the skullduggery we would liked to have presented. According to Milner's private papers his aides through Tavistock contacted a fellow Socialist Fritz Platten. (Milner was a leading Fabian

Socialist although he scorned Sydney and Beatrice Webb.) It was Platten, who planned the logistics of the trip and oversaw it until the revolutionaries arrived in Petrograd.

This was confirmed and borne out by the Wilhelmstrasse Files the majority of which we were able to gain access to, which files were open to certain people qualified to read them. They tallied fairly closely with Bruce Lockhart's account in his private papers as well as what Lord Alfred Milner had to say about the underhand affair that betrayed Russia. It appeared that Milner had many contacts among the Bolshevik expatriates among them, Lenin. It was to Lord Milner that Lenin went, when he needed money for the Revolution. Armed with a letter of introduction from Platten, Lenin met with Lord Milner and laid down his plan for the overthrow of the Romanov's and Christian Russia.

Milner agreed on condition that he could send his agent Bruce Lockhart of MI6 to supervise the day-to-day affairs and report back on Lenin.

Lord Rothschild and the Rockefellers demanded that they be allowed to send Sydney Reilly to Russia to supervise transfer of Russia's natural resources and the gold rubles held in the Central Bank to London. This was agreed to by Lenin, and later Trotsky.

To seal the bargain, Lord Milner, on behalf of the Rothschilds, gave Lenin 60 millions pounds in gold sovereigns while the Rockefellers contributed around $40 million dollars.

Countries in complicity with the "sealed train" affair were Great Britain, Germany, Finland, Switzerland and Sweden. While the United States was not directly involved, it must have been aware of what was going on. After all, on the orders of President Wilson, a brand new American passport was issued to Leon Trotsky, (whose real name was Lev Bronstein) so that he could travel in peace, although Trotsky was not a U.S. citizen.

Lenin and his compatriots were provided with a private well-appointed rail carriage by the top German government functionaries and always kept locked by agreements with stations along the line. Platten was in charge and he laid down the rules for the trip, some of which are listed in the Wilhelmstrasse Files:

> ➢ The carriage was to remain locked for the entire trip.
> ➢ No one could board the carriage without Platten's permission.
> ➢ The train would have extra territorial status. No passports were to be asked at borders.
> ➢ Tickets would be bought at regular prices.
> ➢ No "security issues" to be raised by the military or police of any country en-route.

According to the Wilhelmstrasse Files, the trip was authorized and approved by General Ludendorff and Kaiser Wilhelm. Ludendorff went so far as to say that if Sweden refused to let the Bolsheviks pass, he would guarantee them passage into Russia through the German lines! As it turned out, the Swedish Government raised no objection and neither did the Finnish Government.

One of the notable revolutionaries, who joined the train when it arrived at the German frontier with Switzerland, was Radek, who was to play a leading role in the bloody Bolshevik Revolution. There were some lighter moments too. The Wilhelmstrasse Files describe how the carriage missed its engine at Frankfurt, resulting in it being shunted to and from for about 8 hours.

The party had to de-train in the German Baltic town of Sasnitz where they were accorded "decent accommodation" by the German Government. The Swedish Government kindly gave them ferry transport to Malmo, from where they sailed to Stockholm, where "nice" accommodation awaited the Bolshevik party for an overnight layover and then it was on to the Finnish border.

There, the intrepid Platten left the high-spirited party and the final journey into Russia was made by train to Petrograd. Thus an epic journey that began in Zurich, Switzerland, ended in Petrograd. Lenin had arrived on the scene and Russia was about to be brought low. And throughout, Bernays and Lippmann and their associates at Wellington House (Tavistock) kept up a steady flow of brainwashing propaganda that it is safe to conclude, duped much of the world.

CHAPTER 2

Europe falls off the precipice

Europe after WWI and the close of the Bolshevik Revolution was forced to change according to the Tavistock blueprint. When, thanks to the British engendered and instigated First World War, Europe fell off a precipice into the end of their world, or perhaps it might be more appropriate to say, shambled along like zombies until the last of the era vanished into the darkness of the abyss, the forced changes became very much apparent.

This is not a book about the First World War per se. Hundreds of thousands of words have been written about the cause and effects of the greatest tragedy ever to befall mankind, and yet it has not been adequately addressed and probably never will be. One thing that many writers - myself included - are agreed on.

The war was started by Great Britain out of sheer hated of Germany's rapid progress toward becoming a major economic power in competition against Britain, and Lord Edward Grey was the principle architect of the war.

That it was unpopular and not approved of by a large majority of the British people called for "special measures" a new department to handle the challenge. In essence, that is the reason why Wellington House came into existence.

From such a small beginning, it progressed into the gargantuan Tavistock Institute of Human Relations, by 2005, the world's premier brainwashing institution and a most sinister force. That it will have to be confronted and put out of business if the United

States is to survive as a constitutional Republic with a Republican form of government guaranteed to the 50 States is the considered opinion of a number of members of the U.S. Senate, who were consulted in preparation for this book, but who asked not to be named.

The aftermath of the First World War and the failed attempts to form a League of Nations served only to emphasize the gap between the old Western civilization and the new. The economic disaster of postwar Germany hung like the smoke from a funeral pyre over Western culture adding to the dismal, sad and fearful climate that began in the 1920s.

Historian agree that all of the combatants suffered economic ravage of varying degree, although Russia was somewhat spared, only to be destroyed by the Bolsheviks, while Germany and Austria were the hardest hit. A strange kind of a forced gaiety descended on Europe in the 1920s (in which I include Britain) and the United States. It was put down to "rebellious youth" and people generally being "sick of war and politics." In point of fact, people were reacting to the long-range penetration and inner-directional conditioning of the masters at Tavistock.

In the period between the end of WWI and 1935, they were as much shell-shocked as were the troops who had survived the hell of the trenches with shot and shell flying all around them, only now, it was economic shot and shell and vast changes in social mores that numbed their senses.

But the end result of the "treatment" was the same. People threw discretion to the winds and the moral rot that was set in motion in 1918, is ongoing and gathering momentum. In the state of forced gaiety, nobody saw the coming of the world economic crash and subsequent world depression.

It is agreed by most historians that this condition was engineered and we are led to believe, that Tavistock played a role in the feverish publicity campaigns of various factions in that period. In support of our contention that the crash and depression was a contrived event. See Appendix of Events.

Spengler foretold what was to happen and as it turns out his predictions were amazingly accurate. "Decadent society" and "loose women" characterized by the "flappers", and men in coats fitted with hip flasks, who demanded and got a lessening of female modesty that came in with higher hemlines, bobbed hair and excessive make-up, women smoking and drinking in public. As money became harder to come by and soup kitchen and unemployment lines grew longer, hemlines grew shorter, while the writings of Sinclair Lewis, F. Scott Fitzgerald, James Joyce and D.H. Lawrence drew gasps, the latest Broadway shows and nightclub acts revealed a lot more of women's hidden charms than ever before, and put them out on public display.

It was noted by fashion designers in 1919 in the New Yorker magazine that "hemlines this year are six inches from the ground and very daring."

CHAPTER 3

How "times" were made to change

But that was only the beginning. In 1935 with Hitler rising to power, guaranteed by the impossible conditions forced upon Germany at Versailles, hemlines were also rising to the dizzy height of the knees, except in Germany, where Hitler was demanding modesty from German womanhood and getting it, along with wholesome respect, which did not suit Tavistock's book.

People who stopped to think at all said they hated the way "times are changing," but what they did not and could not know was that times were being made to change according to a carefully laid out Tavistock formula. Everywhere else in Europe and America the revolt was on as "emancipation" fever spread.

In the United States it was silent screen idols who led the way, but this was no match with what was happening in Europe where every single "pleasure" was being indulged in, including homosexuality, that had long been hidden in darkness and never mentioned in polite society.

Homosexuality emerged alongside lesbianism to shock disgust, and it seemed, to deliberately affront those who still lingered in the old order.

A study of this aberration showed that homosexuality and lesbianism became rampant not out of any inner or latent desires, but as a means to "shocking" the old establishment with its rigid codes of good order. Music too suffered and "went to the dogs" in all manner of jazz and other "decadent" forms.

Tavistock was now in the most crucial stage of developing its plan that called for womanhood to be reduced to a lessening standard of morality and of feminine behavior never thought possible. Nations were in a state of numbness, "shell- shocked" by the radical changes forced upon them which seemed impossible to stop, in which a complete absence of female modesty reflected in learned behavioral attitudes that made the 1920s and 1930s, look like a ladies Sunday school teacher's convention. There was no stopping the "sexual revolution" that swept the world during that era and the planned degradation of womanhood that went with it.

Some voices were heard, notably G.K. Chesterton and Oswald Spengler, but it was not enough to blunt the assault launched by the Tavistock Institute that had in effect "declared war on Western civilization." The effects of "long range penetration and inner directional conditioning" were everywhere to be observed. The moral, spiritual, racial, economic, cultural and intellectual bankruptcy we are in the midst of today is not some social phenomenon or the result of something abstract or sociological that just "happened". Rather it was the outcome of a carefully planned Tavistock program.

What we are seeing is not accidental, some aberration of history. Rather it is the end product of a deliberately induced social and moral crisis evident everywhere and in such personages as Mick Jagger, Oprah Winfrey, Britney Spears, "reality" television shows, "music" seemingly an amalgam of every base instinct, Fox News (Faux News,) near pornographic movies in mainstream theaters, advertising in which modesty and decency are cast to the winds, loud uncouth behavior in public places, especially in American restaurants; Katie Curic and a host other of female non-entities suddenly "created" to become highly- paid "television anchors" or talk show hosts, all of whom have been trained to talk in a hard, grating monotonous voices totally lacking in cadence, as if talking through clenched jaws, in a manner that is harsh, strident and hard on the ears. Whereas television news readers and "anchormen" had always been men, suddenly, there were no more than a dozen men in the field.

We see it in non-entity "stars" in the movie industry that churn out movies of an increasingly low cultural standard. We see it also in the glorification of interracial marriages, divorce on demand, abortion, and blatant homosexual and lesbian behavior, in the loss of religious beliefs and in Western civilization family life. Such "stars" are Ellen DeGeneres, who have absolutely no talent and nothing of any cultural value to offer, are held up as models for impressionable young girls who are increasingly on parade with as much as 75 percent of their bodies exposed. We see it in a massive increase in drug addiction and all manner of social evil as in Canada passing a "law" making homosexual and lesbian "marriage" legal under the threadbare guise of "civil rights."

We see it in wholesale corruption of the political system and constitutional mayhem where the House and Senate permits flagrant violations of the highest law in the land, at every level of government and nowhere more so than in the Executive branch of government, where every president since Roosevelt has taken powers to which the President is not entitled. We see it in the illicit taking of war powers by the President when such powers are explicitly denied to the Executive by the U.S. Constitution.

We see it in a new dimension of constitutional disobedience added to an ugly list of "laws" not empowered by the Constitution, one of the most recent and most shocking being the U.S. Supreme Court's blatant exceeding of it powers in breaking down States rights and electing George Bush, the younger as the President. This had to be one of the most savage blows struck against the Constitution in the grossest contravention of the 10th Amendment to the U.S. Constitution in the history of the United States. Yet, so dazed and shell- shocked are the American people that no protest was voiced, no mass demonstrations; no calls for the Supreme Court to be reined in. In this one incident alone, the power of Tavistock's "long range penetration and inner directional conditioning" proved to be a huge triumph.

No, this condition of disintegration of our Republic in which we find ourselves in 2005 did not simply evolve; rather it is the end product of a carefully planned social engineering brainwashing project of immense proportions. The truth is reflected in the death throes of what was once the greatest nation on Earth.

The physiological conditioning papers written by the social scientists at Tavistock are working well. Your reaction is a programmed one. You cannot think in any other way unless you make a supreme effort.

Nor can you take steps to free yourself from this condition unless you can first identify the enemy and his plan for the dissolution of the United States and Europe in particular and the Western world in general. That enemy is called the Tavistock Institute for Human Relations and it has been at war with Western civilization since its earliest days before it found form and substance at Wellington House and from there evolved into its present facilities at Sussex University and the Tavistock Clinic in London. Before I unmasked this institution in 1969, it was unknown in the United States. It is without doubt the world's premier brainwashing social engineering establishment.

We shall see what it achieved in its early days in pre-WWI England and since then in the run-up to WWII and post WWII to the present time. During WWII the Tavistock Institute was headquartered at the British Army Physiological Warfare Division. We have covered its history during its formative years at Wellington House and we now proceed to the pre- World War II and post WWII activities.

CHAPTER 4

Social engineering and the Social scientists

Dr. Kurt Lewin was its chief theoretician who specialized in the teaching and application of topological psychology, which was and remains the most advanced method of behavior modification. Lewin was assisted by Major General John Rawlings Reese, Eric Trist, W.R. Bion, H.V. Dicks and several of the "greats" of brainwashing and social engineering like Margaret Meade and her husband, Gregory Bateson. Bernays was the top consultant right up to the time George Bush was placed in the White House by the Supreme Court. We do not want to get too technical and thus will not get into specifics of how they applied the Social Scientists sciences. Most will accept the generic term of "brainwashing" as an overall explanation of the activities of this, the "mother of all think tanks."

It will come as no small surprise to learn that Lewin and his team founded the Stanford Research Center, the Wharton School of Economics, MIT and the National Institute of Mental Health among scores of other institutions fondly believed to be "American" institutions. During the course of years, the Federal Government contributed millions upon millions of dollars to Tavistock and its expanded web of interlinking institutions, while corporate America and Wall Street came up with matching amounts.

We make bold to say that without the amazing growth and advances techniques for mass brainwashing developed by the Tavistock Institute, there would have been no Second World War, nor any of the wars that followed, and certainly not the two

Gulf Wars, the second of which is still raging in November 2005.

By the year 2000 there was hardly any aspect of life in America into which Tavistock's tentacles had not reached and that included every level of government from local to federal, industry, trade, education and the political institutions of the nation. Every mental and psychological aspect of the nation was analyzed, recorded, profiled and stored in computer memory banks.

What has come out of this is what Tavistock calls "a three-system response" and it is how population groups react to stress resulting from "contrived situations" that become crisis management exercises. What we have in the U.S. and Britain is a government, that creates a situation viewed by its citizens as a crisis, and government then manages that "crisis."

An example of a "contrived situation" was the Japanese attack on Pearl Harbor in December 1941. The attack on Pearl Harbor was "contrived" as previously explained herein with the transfer of Rockefeller cash to Richard Sorge the master spy, and then to a member of the imperial family to prompt Japan to fire the first shots so that the Roosevelt administration could take the United States into WWII.

The economic strangulation of Japan by Britain and the United States unilaterally choking off the flow of essential raw materials to the island factory that was Japan, had reached a point where a decision was made to put an end to it.

Tavistock played an enormous role in crafting the massive wave of anti-Japanese propaganda that swept the United States into the war in Europe via war against Japan.

Unbearable economic pressure was put on Japan while at the same time the Roosevelt administration refused to "negotiate," until the Tokyo government could see no way out but to attack at

Pearl Harbor. Roosevelt had conveniently obligingly shifted the Pacific Fleet into harm's way by moving it from its safe-haven at San Diego to Pearl Harbor, for absolutely no valid or strategic reason, thereby placing it squarely in reach of the Japanese Navy.

Another example is more recent; the Gulf War that began when a hue and a cry was raised about Iraq's alleged stocks of nuclear and chemical weapons, the so-called "weapons of mass destruction," (WMD's.) The Bush administration and the Blair government knew the issue was a "contrived situation" without foundation or merit; they knew that there were no such weapons. Indisputable proof existed that Hussein's weapons program had been nullified after the 1991 Gulf War and through continued brutal sanctions.

In short, the two Western "leaders" were caught out in a web of lies, yet such is the power of the Committee of 300 and the brainwashing power of Tavistock, that they remained in office although it is an accepted fact that because of their lies, at least one million Iraqis and more than 2000 American servicemen dead and 25,999 wounded (Russia's GRU Military Intelligence figures) of which 53 percent are maimed, with the cost in monetary terms as of October 2005, exceeding $550 billion.

The Iraqi death toll is the total of both Gulf Wars of which the majority are civilians who died from the lack of food, clean water and medicine as a result of the criminal sanctions imposed by the British and U.S. Governments under cover of the U.N.

In carrying out sanctions against Iraq, the U.N. violated its own charter and from then on became a crippled institution lacking credibility.

There is no parallel in history where a man holding the highest office was proved to be a liar and deceiver and yet could remain in power as if nothing had stained his office, a state of affairs that demonstrates the power of the Tavistock Institute's "long range penetration and inner conditioning" treatment of the American people, that would cause them docilely to accept such a turgid, horror-filled situation without ever taking to the streets in rage.

Well did Henry Ford say that "people deserve the government they get" if the people do nothing to turn that government out of office, such as is the right of the American people under their U.S. Constitution, then they deserve to have liars and deceivers running their nation and their lives.

On the other hand, the American people may well be going through the one of the three phases of what Dr. Fred Emery, at one time the senior psychiatrist at Tavistock, once described as "social environmental turbulence." According to Emery: "Large populations groups manifest the following symptoms when subjected to conditions of violent social changes, stress and turbulence which can be divided into well-defined categories:

Superficiality is the condition that manifests itself when the threatened population group reacts by adopting shallow sloganeering, which they attempt to pass off as ideals."

Very little "ego investment" takes place making the first phase a "maladaptive response" because, as Emery stated, "the cause of the crisis is not isolated and identified" and the crisis and tension is not abated, but continues for as long as the controller want it to last. The second phase of the crisis reaction (since the crisis is continuing), is "fragmentation", a condition in which panic strikes, "social cohesion" falls apart with the result that very small groups form and attempt to protect themselves from the crisis with little or no regard for the expense or cost to other fragmented, small groups. This phase Emery calls "passive maladaption," while still failing to identify the cause of the crisis.

The third phase is when the victims turn away from the source of the induced crisis and the resulting tension. They take "fantasy trips of internal migration, introspection and obsession with self."

This is what Tavistock calls "disassociation and self realization." Emery goes on to explain that "the passive maladaption responses are now coupled with "active maladaptive responses."

Emery states that over the past 50 years that experiments in applied social psychology and resultant "crisis management" have taken over all aspects of life in America and the results are stored in the computers in the major "think tanks" such as Stanford University. The scenarios are taken out, used and revised from time to time and, according to Tavistock, "the scenarios are in operation at the present time."

Translated this means that Tavistock has the majority of the American people profiled and brainwashed. If any part of the American public is ever able to identify the cause of the crises that have washed over this nation in the past seventy years, the social engineering structure built by Tavistock will come crashing down. But that has not yet happened. Tavistock continues to drown the American public in its sea of created public opinion.

The social engineering developed by the Social Sciences scientists at Tavistock has been used as a weapon during this century's two world wars, especially World War I. The pollsters who developed it have been quite frank that they employ on the American population the same devices and methods used and experimented with against enemy populations.

Today, the manipulation-by-polls of public opinion has become a central technique in the hands of the social engineers and controllers of the Social scientists employed at Tavistock and its many "think tanks" located all over the United States and Britain.

CHAPTER 5

Do we have what H.G. Wells called "An Invisible Government?"

As I have previously related, the modern science of making public opinion through advanced techniques of manipulating mass-opinion began at one of the West's most advanced propaganda factory situated in Britain at Wellington House. This facility dedicated to social engineering and creating public opinion at the commencement of World War I, was under the aegis of Lords Rothmere and Northcliffe, and the future director of studies of the Royal Institute of International Affairs (RIIA), Arnold Toynbee. Wellington House had an American Section, whose most prominent members were Walter Lippmann and Edward Bernays. As we discovered later, Bernays was the nephew of Sigmund Freud, a fact carefully hidden from public view.

Jointly, they centered work on techniques to "mobilize" support for World War I among the masses of people who were opposed to war with Germany. The public perception was that Germany was a friend of the British people, not an enemy and the British people saw no need to fight Germany. After all, was it not true that Queen Victoria was the cousin of Kaiser Wilhelm II? Toynbee, Lippmann and Bernays worked to persuade them that war was necessary, using the techniques of the new science through new arts of mass-manipulation via the communications media for its propaganda purposes tinged with willingness to lie, which was just getting into its stride, having learned a great deal of experience during the Anglo-Boer War (1899-1902).

It was not only the British public whose perception of events had to be altered, but also a recalcitrant American public.

To this end Bernays and Lippmann were instrumental in getting Woodrow Wilson to establish the Creel Committee, which created the first body of methodological techniques for dissemination of successful propaganda and for the science of polling to secure the "correct" opinion.

From the beginning the techniques were designed in such a way that polling (public opinion-making) was based on one obvious, but striking feature: — it was concerned with people's opinions, not with their understanding of the processes of science. Thus, by intent, the pollsters elevated an essentially irrational element of mind to a primary level of public focus. This was a conscious decision to undermine the grasps of reality of masses of people in an increasingly complex industrial society.

If you have ever watched "Fox News" where viewers are given the results of a poll about "what Americans are thinking," and then for the next hour found yourself shaking your head and wondering what the results of the poll reflected about your own thinking processes, then you could only have felt more puzzled than ever.

The key to understanding Fox News and the poll might lie in what Lippmann had to say about such matters. In his 1922 book, Public Opinion, Lippmann outlined Tavistock's psychological warfare methodology.

In an introductory chapter, "The World Outside and the Pictures in Our Heads," Lippmann stressed, "that the object of study of the public opinion social analyst is reality as defined by internal perception or images of that reality. Public opinion deals with indirect, unseen, and puzzling facts, and there is nothing obvious about them. The situations to which public opinions refer are known only as opinions"

"The pictures inside the heads of these human beings, the pictures of themselves, of others, of their needs, purposes, and relationship, are their public opinions. Those pictures, which are acted upon by groups of people, or by individuals acting in the name of groups, are Public Opinion with capital letters. The picture inside so often misleads men in their dealings with the world outside."

From this evaluation, it is easy to take the next decisive step made by Bernays, — that the elites who run society can and do marshal the resources of mass communications to mobilize and alter the "herd" mind.

One year after Lippmann's book, Bernays authored Crystallizing Public Opinion. He followed that in 1928 with a book entitled quite simply: Propaganda.

In the first chapter, "Organizing Chaos" Bernays wrote: The conscious and intelligent manipulation of the organized, habits and opinions of the masses is an important element in democratic society. Those who manipulate this unseen mechanism of society constitute an invisible government, which is the true ruling power of our country.

We are governed, our minds are molded, our tastes formed, our ideas-suggested, largely by men, that we have never heard of... Our invisible governors are, in many cases, unaware of the identity of their fellow members in the inner cabinet.

Whatever attitude one chooses to take toward this condition, it remains a fact that in almost every act of our daily lives, whether in the sphere of politics or business, in our social conductor or our ethical thinking, we are dominated by the relatively small number of persons—a trifling fraction of our hundred arid twenty million—who understand the mental processes and social patterns of the masses. It is they who pull the wires, which control the public mind, who harness old social forces and contrive new ways to bind and guide the world.

In Propaganda, Bernays followed his praise of the "invisible government" by underscoring the next phase that propaganda techniques would follow:

As civilization has become more complex, and as the need for invisible government has been increasingly demonstrated, the technical means have been invented and developed by which opinion may be regimented. With the printing press and the newspaper, the telephone, telegraph, radio and airplanes, ideas can spread rapidly and even instantaneously over the whole of America.

To back up his point, Bernays quoted the mentor of "public opinion manipulation," H. G. Wells. He cited a 1928 article in the New York Times in which Wells welcomed "modern means of communication" for "opening up a new world of political processes," and for allowing "the common design" to be "documented and sustained against perversion and betrayal." For Wells, the advent of "mass communication" leading up to television meant fantastic new paths for social control beyond the wildest dreams of the earlier mass- manipulation fanatics of the British Fabian Society. We shall return to this vitally important subject later herein.

CHAPTER 6

Mass communications ushers in the polling industry

For Bernays, his recognition of Wells' idea won him a key place in the hierarchy of U.S. public opinion controllers; in 1929, he won a position at CBS, which had recently been taken over by William Paley.

By the same token, the advent of mass communications ushered in the polling/sampling industry, to organize the perceptions of the masses for the media mafia (part of the "invisible government" running the show from behind the scenes.)

By 1935-36, polling was in full swing. In the same year, Elmo Roper began his Fortune magazine FOR surveys, which evolved into his "What People Are Thinking" column for the New York Herald Tribune.

George Gallup initiated the American Institute of Public Opinion; — in 1936 he opened up the British Institute of Public Opinion. Gallup was to headquarter his activities around Princeton University, intermeshing with the Office of Public Opinion Research/Institute for International Social Research/Psychology Department complex run by Hadley Cantril, who was destined to play an increasingly important role in developing the psychological profiling methods later to be used in manufacturing the Aquarian Conspiracy.

In the same 1935-36 period, the first-time use was made of polling in presidential elections, under the impetus of two newspapers owned by the Cowles family, the Minneapolis Star-Tribune and the Des Moines Register. The Cowles are still in the news business.

Based in Spokane, Washington, they are active opinion makers and their support of the Bush war in Iraq was a crucial factor.

It is not certain who introduced the practice of "advisors to the President," - those persons who are not elected by the citizens and whom they have no opportunity to vet, but who decided the internal and external foreign policies of the Nation. Woodrow Wilson was the first American President to make use of the practice.

Opinion Research and World War II

These were all small lead-ups to the next phase, triggered by two important intersecting developments: the arrival of emigre psychological warfare expert Kurt Lewin in Iowa, and the involvement of the United States in World War II.

World War II provided the emerging Tavistock Social sciences scientists with enormous scope for experimentation. Lewin's leadership put together the key-force that would deploy after World War II to utilize those techniques developed in warfare against the population of the United States. In fact in 1946, Tavistock declared war on the civilian population of the United States and has remained in a state of war ever since.

The basic conceptions expounded by Lewin, Wells, Bernays, and Lippmann remained in place as the guidepost for manipulation of public opinion; the war gave the Social scientists the opportunity to apply them in highly concentrated form and to bring together a large number of institutions under their direction to further the ends of their experiments.

The core institute which was the vehicle for making "public

opinion," was the Committee on National Morale. Ostensibly established to mobilize support for the war in much as President Wilson had set up his management committee to "manage" WWI, its real purpose was to carry out the intensive profiling of both the "Axis" and Americans population for the purposes of creating and maintaining a means of social control.

The committee was headed by several leaders of American society, including Robert P. Bass, Herbert Bayard Swope, among other notables. Its secretary was Margaret Meade's husband, Gregory Bateson, one of the principal instigators of the CIA's notorious "MK-Ultra" LSD experiments that some experts consider as the launch vehicle for the U.S. counterculture of drugs, rock and sex.

The committee's Board of Trustees included poll-taker George Gallup; intelligence agent Ladislas Farago and Tavistock psychologist, Gardner Murphy.

The committee ran a number of special projects, the most important being a major study on how best to wage Psychological Warfare on Germany. The key personnel critical to the development of the public opinion project were:

- Kurt K. Lewin, Education and History; Psychology; Social Sciences
- Professor Gordon W. Allport, Psychology
- Professor Edwin G. Borin, Psychology
- Professor Hadley Cantril, Psychology
- Ronald Lippitt, Social Sciences
- Margaret Mead, Anthropology, Social Sciences; Youth & Child Development

The staff numbered more than a 100 researchers who comprised the staff of the Committee, and several opinion-profiling institutions critical to the project.

One such a special project team was in the Office and Strategic Services (OSS) (the forerunner of the CIA) composed of Margaret Mead, Kurt Lewin, Ronald Lippitt, Dorwin Cartwright, John K. French and public-opinion makers like Samuel Stouffer (later chairman of the Laboratory Social Relations group at Harvard University); Paul Lazarsfeld of Columbia University's Sociology Department, who developed with profiler Harold Lasswell an "opinion research" methodology for the OSS based on detailed "content analysis" of the local press of enemy countries and Rensis Likert.

Likert, a Prudential Insurance Company key executive immediately before the war, had perfected profiling techniques as the director of research for the Life Insurance Agency Management Association. This equipped him to interact favorably with the head of the U.S. Strategic Bombing Survey, who was the former head of Prudential Life Insurance Company. Likert served as director of the division of morale of the Strategic Bombing Survey from 1945-1946 from which position he had enormous scope for mass public opinion profiling and manipulation.

CHAPTER 7

The making of public opinion

According to Tavistock Institute records, the Strategic Bombing Survey played a key role in forcing Germany to its knees through a highly disciplined program of systematic bombing of German worker housing, which Sir Arthur Harris of the RAF was only too delighted to carry out.

In addition, from 1939-1945, Likert ran the Division of Program Surveys of the Department of Agriculture, from which major studies were undertaken in the techniques of "mass persuasion." Or to put it another way, "making public opinion to fit the desired goals." One can only speculate on the numbers of citizens who believed their support for the "Allied" war effort sprang from their own opinions.

One of Likert's key aides in the division was Lewin protege and future Tavistock operative Dorwin Cartwright, who wrote the text-book document titled, "Some Principles of Mass Persuasion " which is still in use today.

Another major agency for shaping public opinion was the Office of War Information, directed by Gardner Cowles for much of the war effort. Bernays was brought into OWI as an advisor. It is out of the nexus we have described here that the network of key "polling institutions" emerged after World War II. They have played a powerful and decisive role in American life ever since. Gallup, from the committee on National Morale's Board of Trustees, upgraded his activity and became the key commander of polling institutions for launching new policies of the

Committee of 300, which he passed off as "polling results."

Bernays played several key postwar roles. In 1953, he wrote a paper for the State Department that recommended setting up a psychological warfare office by State. In 1954, he was a consultant to the U.S. Air Force, the armed forces branch most under the influence of the Strategic Bombing Survey people.

During this early 1950s period, Bernays was public relations counsel to the United Fruit (United Brands) Corporation, one of the leading corporations in the communication/national security apparat (Eisenhower's "military-industrial complex") then busy with consolidating its power over U.S. policy.

Bernays conducted the propaganda campaign alleging Guatemala was falling under "Communist control" that resulted in a U.S. engineered coup in that country. In 1955 Bernays wrote a book about his experience titled "The Engineering of Consent."

The book became the virtual Tavistock blueprint followed by the U.S. Government to overthrow any country whose policies were unacceptable to the One World Government Socialist dictatorship.

Throughout the postwar period, Bernays was a member of the Society for Applied Anthropology, one of Margaret Mead's social-control institutions inside the U.S., and the Society for the Psychological Study of Social Issues, a group created by John Rawlings Reese, a founder member of Tavistock to run "psychiatric shock troops" among the American population.

One of its first actions was the unlashing of homosexuality in Florida, a move bitterly opposed by Anita Bryant who had no idea of what she was up against.

The second of its actions was to introduce the theme that non-white people are more intelligent than whites, which we shall discuss later.

Likert moved to the University of Michigan to set up the Institute
for Social Research (ISR) that absorbed the Massachusetts
Center for the Study of Group Dynamics, the principal Tavistock
affiliate in the U.S. in the beginning of the postwar era.

Tavistock's ISR was the center of a number of critical profiling
and "Opinion Research" subgroups, among them the Center for
research in the Utilization of Scientific Knowledge, was
established by Likert OSS co-worker and Lewin disciples,
Ronald Lippitt.

Project Director Donald Michael was a leading player in the Club
of Rome, and a second subgroup, the Survey Research Center,
was Likert's own personal creation that grew to become the most
elaborate institution in the U.S. for "surveying" (creating)
popular attitudes and trends, among the principal of which were
demeaning and degrading womanhood and pushing the superior
intellectual capabilities of non-white persons according to
Lewin's carefully crafted scripts.

Robert Hutchins became famous during this period and his
closest colleague in those early years was William Benton, the
founder in 1929 with Chester Bowles of Benton and Bowles, the
well-known advertising firm. Benton utilized Benton and Bowles
as a means to develop the science of mass control through
advertising.

It was Benton's pioneering work supported by Douglass Cater,
that led to the development of Tavistock's burgeoning control
over U.S. media policy through the Aspen Institute of Colorado,
the American home of the Socialist One World Government
Committee of 300.

In passing I mention that the science of mass media control
through advertising is today so firmly entrenched that it has

become the key component in opinion making. In the early post WWII days, Hollywood incorporated it into nearly all of its movies.

Advertising (brainwashing) was done through the type and make of car the hero drove, the brand of cigarette the suave Lawrence Harvey smoked, the clothes and make up the leading lady wore, clothes that became more risque with each passing year, until today in 2005 we have womanhood degraded by the likes of Britney Spear's almost naked breasts and bare stomach exposed by crotch hugging jeans she often wears, the social mores that Hollywood enjoys so much in flouting.

CHAPTER 8

Degrading women and decline of moral standards

The pace of degrading womanhood has quickened at a remarkable degree since hemlines reached the knee. This is manifesting itself in such areas as near pornography in mainstream movies and soap operas and we venture to suggest that the day is not far off, when such scenes will be "total and mandatory."

This decline in attractive feminine speech can be traced to Tavistock methodology and its practitioners, Cantril, Likert and Lewin. Another noticeable change was the increase in movies featuring inter-racial dating and sexual encounters coupled with "human rights" claims for lesbians in the most blatantly open form.

Special people were selected and trained for this task, probably the best known of many being Ellen Degeneres who received hundreds of thousands of dollars worth of free publicity under the guise of being interviewed on talk shows and "discussion" groups on the subject of "same-sex love" meaning encounters between two females involving a type of sex practice.

Benton the pioneer in degrading womanhood had as his mentor Social scientist's leading expert in profiling theory at Tavistock, one Harold Lasswell, who together with Benton founded the American Policy Commission in 1940. Lasswell's joint venture with Benton marked the clearest link between Aspen's hidden Socialist One World Government operations in America and the

Tavistock Institute. Aspen became the headquarters of the Committee of 300 branches in the United States.

Hedley Cantril, Likert and Lewin with their humanistic psychology brainwashing applied methodology, played an increasingly vital role in using "opinion research" to bring about paradigm shifts value shifts in society, such as those just described, but on an expanded range and reaching into every level of society that comprised Western civilization as it had been known for centuries.

Cantril's home base from where he conducted his war operations against the American people was the Office of Public Opinion Research at Princeton University, founded in 1940, the same year in which Cantril wrote his book entitled, The Invasion From Mars, a detailed analysis about how the population of the New York-New Jersey area reacted with fear and panic to Orson Wells "War of the Worlds" broadcast in 1938.

How could they have known that they were part of a profiling venture since it is reasonable to conclude that in 1938 not one in five million had ever heard of Hadley Cantril or the Tavistock Institute. It would be interesting to find out how many Americans have heard of Tavistock now in 2005?

Most would remember Orson Wells, but the probabilities are that ninety-nine percent of the population would not attach any significance to the name, Cantril, or have any knowledge of the Tavistock Institute.

Let us recount the events of the night of October 30th 1938, because the same techniques have been used by the Bush Administration, the Defense Department and the CIA to shape the public perception of the events that led up to the invasion of Iraq in 2003 and are still very much in use in 2005.

In 1938, Orson Wells had created quite a reputation for himself as a master at staging faux news events by making use of the English author, H.G. Wells, a former MI6 operative and his book, The War of the Worlds.

In the radio adaptation of the Wells' work, the other Wells, interrupted radio programs in New Jersey with an announcement that Martians had just landed. "The Martian invasion has begun," said Orson Wells.

During the 4-hour long production, it was announced no less than four times that what radio audiences were listening to was a fictitious re-enactment of what it would be like if H.G. Wells' story had come to life. But that availed nothing. Panic gripped millions of people who fled from their homes in terror, jamming roads and communication systems.

What was the purpose of the "hoax?" In the first instance it was to gauge just how effective Cantril and Tavistock's methods were in practice, and perhaps of greater importance, it was to set the stage for the coming war in Europe in which "news broadcasts" would play a crucial role in information gathering and dissemination as an established source of reliable information, as well as a forum for directing public opinion.

Two days after the "Martian Invasion news broadcast," an editorial in the New York Times headed "Terror by Radio" inadvertently shed light on what Tavistock had in mind for the American people in the coming war now looming closer: "What began as entertainment might readily have ended in disaster," the editorial said. Radio officials had a responsibility and "should think twice before mingling news techniques with fiction so terrifying."

What the "Times" had inadvertently stumbled onto was the wave of the future seen through the eyes of the theoreticians at Tavistock. Henceforth, "mingling news techniques with fiction so terrifying" that it would be taken as fact, was to be standard practice for the graduates of Tavistock. All news broadcast were to be adaptations of "news and fiction" in a skilful blend so as to make the one unrecognizable from the other.

In fact, Tavistock put their newly tested theory into practice a year later when the population of cities in Europe, London, Munich, Paris and Amsterdam were smitten with war jitters even as Neville Chamberlain was successfully avoiding war, using the same techniques that were employed in the October 1938 "War of the Worlds" radio broadcasts.

CHAPTER 9

How individuals and groups react to blending fact with fiction

Cantril's conclusion was that the public reacted exactly as his profiling research experiments had led him to believe it would. That Sunday night October 30, 1938 was to become a landmark date in his files and a date signifying a vast paradigm shift for ever in the way that "news" would henceforth, be presented. Slightly more than seven decades later, the world is still being fed a diet of news mingled with fiction, - fiction that in so many instances is terrifying. The Western world has undergone drastic changes unwillingly forced upon it, that it has become a world so vastly different from what it was on that October night in 1938, as to be "another planet." We shall return to this vital subject later in this work.

Following the Second World War, Cantril became totally involved with the head guru at Tavistock, its founder, John Rawlings Reese and his World Tensions Project at the United Nations' UNESCO.

Profiles on how individuals and groups reacted to international tensions were formulated on the basis of skillfully blending fact with terrifying fiction in preparation for a campaign to launch "World citizens," (of a One World Government Socialist-Communist dictatorship) that began to be employed to weaken national boundaries, language and culture and to discredit pride of nation and sovereignty of nation-states, in preparation for the coming of the Socialist New World Order—One World Government, that President Woodrow Wilson said America would make safe for "democracy."

Those fresh-faced young American boys from Arkansas and North Carolina were sent marching off to Europe believing they were "fighting for their country," never knowing that the "democracy" Wilson sent them to "make safe for the world" was a Socialist-International Communist One World Government dictatorship.

John Rawlings Reese was the publisher of Tavistock's magazine Journal of Humanistic Psychology. Their joint thinking mentality is seen in the 1955 monograph, "Toward a Humanistic Psychology, " an as a progression of Cantril's support for the Tavistock-trained Gordon Airport's perception of the "personality." As he expressed it in the 1947 book, Understanding Man's Social Behavior, in a chapter on "Causality." Cantril's methodology was based on the conception that "the particular environment in which growth takes place gives the particular individual a particular direction for growth."

Cantril's endeavors are good examples of the breakdown of boundaries between supposedly neutral opinion taking and social-engineering opinion making;

Tavistock's commitment to forcing major shifts in personality and behavior in all sectors of targeted population groups such as we have sought to describe.

Cantril appointed a board of directors to assist in the work, among who were:

> Warren Bennis, a follower of Tavistock director Eric Trist.

> Marilyn Ferguson, allegedly the author of The Aquarian Conspiracy;

> Jean Houston, head of the Institute for Brain Research,

member of the Club of Rome and author of Mind Games.

> Aldous Huxley, who supervised the MK-Ultra LSD program that ran for 20 years.

> Willis Harman, a Stanford University director and mentor of "The Changing Images of Man" later disguised as "The Aquarian Conspiracy" passed off as the work of Marilyn Ferguson.

> Michael Murphy, head of the Esalen Institute, established by Huxley and others as the Center for "sensitivity training" and drug experiments.

> James F.T. Bugenthal, an initiator of cult-creation projects at Esalen.

> Abraham Maslow, the leading exponent of the irrationalist "think force" and founder of AHP in 1957.

> Carl Rogers, Maslow's co-worker at the AHP in 1957.

AHP's reigning ideology was exemplified by a book review in a 1966 issue of its journal, The Journal of Humanistic Psychology.

Reviewing Maslow's book, The Psychology of Science, Willis Harman, a year before his 1967-69 Stanford Research study, welcomed the "challenge to science" from "extrasensory perception, psycho kinesis, mysticism, and consciousness-expanding drugs" (particularly LSD and Mesacalin.) He lauded Maslow's "new science" since it would bring to the fore "hypnosis, creativity, parapsychology, and psychedelic experience," and shift scientific concern away from the "outside" world to studying "inner space."

This was Cantril's original "particular personality" thinking brought to its logical conclusion. To Cantril goes the "glory and honor" of forcing a vast paradigm shift on the way the Western world thinks and behaves.

Certainly Oswald Spengler would have had no trouble in identifying it as one of the causes of the downfall of the West he had predicted in 1936.

Making Changes in the "Cognitive and Behavioral Structure."

Whatever the particular coloration of ideology that accompanied the scientists of the polling institutions after World War II, the invariant notion of social engineering trough "sampling methods" and "opinion research" could be found in Cartwright's paper Some Principles of Mass Persuasion prepared for the Division of Program Surveys of the Department of Agriculture.

The paper was subtitled, "Selected Findings of Research on the Sale of United States War Bonds," but as Cartwright makes clear, the war-related aspect of the survey was just a pretext for conducting an analysis on the principles of how perception can be modified to suit whatever ends the controller might have in mind.

One would be puzzled as to what the sale of war bonds had to do with agriculture, but that was part of Cartwright's methodology. It was the Bernays-Lippmann-Cantril-Cartwright hypothesis synthesized and concentrated in a World War II setting. The article was featured in Tavistock's journal. Human Relations which ought to immediately brought the reader to attention.

"Among the many technological advances of the past century that have produced changes in social organization," Cartwright began, "the development of the mass media of communication promises to be the most far reaching. This heightened interdependence of people means that the possibilities of mobilizing mass social action have been greatly increased. It is conceivable that one persuasive person could, through the use of mass media, bend the world's population to his will." We do not believe that Cartwright had Jesus Christ in mind when he made that statement.

Under a subheading, "Creating a Particular Cognitive Structure," Cartwright continues:

Principle One: "It is considered a truism by virtually all psychologists that a person's behavior is guided by his perception of the world in which he lives.... It follows from this formulation that one way to change a person's behavior is to modify his cognitive structure. The modification of cognitive structure in individuals by means of the mass media has several prerequisites. These may be stated in the form of principles."

Interspersing his account with examples from the application of his study to the World War Two war-bonds sale drive, Cartwright then elaborated the principles: "The 'message' (i.e., information, facts, etc.), must reach the sense organs of the persons who are to be influenced... Total stimulus situations are selected or rejected on the basis of an impression of their general characteristics," etc. A second set of principles investigated more deeply the methods of altering "cognitive structure."

Principle Two: "Having reached the sense organs, 'message' must be accepted as part of the person's cognitive structure." Cartwright noted in this section that "any effort to change behavior through a modification of this cognitive structure must overcome the forces tending to maintain the present structure.

Only when a given cognitive structure seems to the person to be unsatisfactory for his adjustment is he likely readily to receive influences designed to change that structure."

Under "Creating a Particular Motivational Structure," Cartwright analyzed further "the social inductions the governors of the U.S. Federal Reserve System in Washington into turmoil for a protracted period."

CHAPTER 10

Polling comes of age

The Tavistock Clinic in London was where Sigmund Freud had settled when he arrived from Germany, and where his nephew, Edward Bernays later held court.

Thus it was that England became the world's center for mass brainwashing, social engineering experimenting that spread to postwar clinics spread all over the United States.

During World War II, Tavistock was the headquarters of the British Army's Psychological Warfare Bureau which, through the arrangements of the British Special Operation Executive (SOE) (later known as MI6) dictated policy to the United States Armed Forces in matters of psychological warfare.

Toward the end of the war, Tavistock personnel took over the World Federation of Mental Health and the Psychological Warfare Division of the Supreme Headquarters, Allied Expeditionary Force (SHAEF) in Europe.

Tavistock's chief theoretician, Dr. Kurt Lewin, came to the United States to organize the Harvard Psychological Clinic, the MIT research Center for Groups Dynamics, the Institute of Social Research at the University of Michigan; while his colleagues, Cartwright and Cantrill joined him to play a pivotal policy role at the psychological department of the Office of Strategic Services (OSS), the Office of Naval Research ONI), the U.S. Strategic Bombing Survey and the Committee of National Morale.

Moreover, a large number of influential people at top policy levels were trained in Dr. Lewin's theory of topological psychology, which is to this day the worlds most advanced method of behavior modification-brainwashing. Important colleagues of Kurt Lewin at Tavistock, Eric Trist, John Rawlings Reese, H.V. Dicks, W.R. Bion and Richard Crossman plus selected personnel from the Strategic Bombing Survey, the Committee on National Morale and the National Defense Resources Council, joined Lewin at Rand Corporation, the Stanford Research Institute, the Wharton School, the National Training Laboratories and the National Institute of Mental Health.

The United States government began contracting multimillion-dollar projects with all these institutions. Over a period of the forty years, tens of billions of dollars have been allocated by the Federal Government to fund the work of these groups; while additional tens of billions of dollars found their way into these institutions from private foundations.

As years passed, these institutions grew and the scope of projects they contracted grew with them. Every aspect of the mental and psychological life of the American people was profiled, recorded and stored into computer memory banks.

The institutions, personnel and networks kept on expanding and penetrating deeply into every nook and cranny of Federal, State and Local governments. Their in-house specialists and graduates were called in to develop policies for welfare departments, labor mediation boards, trade unions, the Air Force, the Navy, the Army, the National Education Association and psychiatric clinics, and the White House, the Defense Department and the State Department. It also has extensive contracts with the Central Intelligence Agency (CIA).

Close cooperative relations were developed between these think-tanks and the U.S.A.'s key polling organizations and the major media companies. Gallup Poll, the Yankelovich - CBS-New York Times poll, the National Opinion Research Center and others incessantly conducted psychological profiles of the entire population, sharing the results for evaluation and processing with the ubiquitous social psychologists.

What the public sees in newspapers as opinion polls represents only a fractional portion of the work that the pollsters undertook to do. A key to the control of Tavistock over key sectors of the daily business of government in the U.S. is that it now has its own de-facto television outlet in Fox News, since its acquisition by Richard Murdoch, a virtual seamless propaganda machine for the government.

Above this closely knit grouping of social psychologists, pollsters and media manipulators, presides an elite of powerful patrons, "the Gods of Olympus" (the Committee of 300). It is known in informed circles, that the group controls everything in the world with the exception of Russia and latterly, China.

It plans and acts out long-term strategies in a totally, disciplined and unified manner. It commands over 400 of the top Fortune 500 companies in the U.S. with interlocking connections that reach into every facet of government, trade, banking, foreign policy, intelligence agencies and the military establishment.

It has absorbed all the other "power groups" of earlier U.S. history; the Rothschild, Morgan, Rockefeller group, the Eastern Liberal Establishment personified by the Perkins, Cabot, Lodge families, the creme of the old East India opium trade that generated billions of dollars.

Its hierarchy comprises the old families descended from the British East India Company with its vast fortunes derived from the opium trade that is run from the top down, including European royalty among others.

In the deeper recesses of the intelligence establishment in Washington, veteran intelligence officers refer to this awesome group, in hushed tones and mysterious language as the "Committee of 300." The leaders are called "The Olympians." No U.S. president is elected or remains in office save and except by their favor.

Those who buck their control are removed. Examples are John F. Kennedy, Richard Nixon and Lyndon Johnson. The Committee of 300 is the international Socialist One World Government that runs the New World Order from behind the scenes where it will remain, until it is ready to emerge and take open and full control of all governments of the world in an International Communist dictatorship.

CHAPTER 11

The paradigm shift in education

During the 1970s a dramatic paradigm shift in school curricula at all levels came into effect apparently to the point that students were awarded school credits for courses in civics instead of reading, writing and arithmetic. An epidemic of "casual sex" and drug-taking overwhelmed school-age teens and swept over the entire country.

In July 1980, a major international conference was held in Toronto, Canada, under the auspices of First Global Conference on the Future in which 4,000 social engineers, cybernetics experts and futurologists from all the think tanks participated. The conference was under the direction of the Tavistock Institute's billionaire chairman, Maurice Strong who set the theme:

"The time has come to move from thinking and dialogue to action. This conference will become the launching pad for that important action to occur in the 1980s."

Strong was chairman of Petro-Canada, one of several "flagship" companies of the "Olympians." His background was British Intelligence MI6 where he held the rank of colonel during World War II. Strong and his network of companies were heavily involved in the highly lucrative opium-heroin-cocaine trade. Strong and Aldous Huxley were responsible for the LSD plague that swept the United States and later, Europe. He was a former director of the United Nations Environmental Program.

One of the chief speakers for the "Olympians" at the conference was Dr. Aurelio Peccei, chairman of the Club of Rome, a NATO think tank.

The North Atlantic Treaty Organization (NATO) was created within the framework of the Aquarian Conspiracy, a project by the Social scientists at Stanford University under the direction of Willis Harmon. NATO in turn formed and promoted a new branch called "The Club of Rome," the name being designed to confuse and dissemble as it had nothing to do with the Catholic Church.

Without going into the technicalities of the Club of Rome, (hereinafter referred to as "the Club,") its purpose was to act as a counterweight against post-industrial agricultural and military expansion, a so-called "post-industrial agricultural zero growth society," which was meant to halt America's burgeoning manufacturing industries and growing mechanized farming food production capability. Memberships of the Club and NATO were interchangeable.

Stanford Research, the Tavistock Institute and other centers of applied social psychiatry joined it. In 1994 Tavistock signed a major contract with NASA to evaluate the effects of its space program. The Club itself was only founded in 1968 as part of the call for a New World Order inside a One World Government. What the Club became was an instrument to enforce limits of growth on industrial nations, and the United States was the first country to be targeted.

This was in fact one of the earliest steps taken to implement the "300" goal of returning the U.S. to a state of feudalism, a feudal society. One of the industries the Club railed against was nuclear energy, and they were successful in halting construction of all nuclear electricity generating plants that has put demand a thousand years ahead of the supply of electrical power. NATO was its military alliance meant to keep Russia in line.

On the agenda of the 1980 meeting referred to above were the following:

- ➢ Women's liberation movement.

- ➢ Black consciousness, racial mixing, breaking down taboos against mixed marriages as propounded by anthropologist Margaret Meade and Gregory Bateson of Tavistock.

- ➢ It was decided at this meeting that an aggressive program would be launched to portray "colored races" as superior to Western Civilization white persons. From this forum came Oprah Winfrey and a host of black persons who were picked up and trained for their roles to portray "mixed races" as superior to whites.

- ➢ It could also be seen in movies where black movie stars suddenly proliferated until they became household names. It was seen also where a black person was placed in the role a high position of authority over whites, such a judge, or a district head of the FBI and the military, CEOs of large corporations etc.

- ➢ Youth rebellion against imagined societal wrongs.

- ➢ Emerging interest in social responsibility of business.

- ➢ The generation gap implying a changing paradigm.

- ➢ The anti-technological bias of many young people.

- ➢ Experimentation with new family structures interpersonal relationships in which homosexuality and lesbianism became "normalized" and "no different from other people acceptable at all levels of society, two lesbian "moms."

- ➢ The emergence of the fake conservation/ecology movements such as "Greenpeace"

- ➢ A surge in interest in Eastern religious and philosophical perspectives.

➢ A renewed interest in "fundamentalist" Christianity.

➢ Labor unions shifting emphasis to quality of the work environment.

➢ An increasing interest in meditation and other spiritual disciplines The "Kabala" was to supplant Christian culture and special people were chosen to teach and spread Kabala. Early chosen disciples were Shirley McLean, Roseanne Barr and later, Madonna and Demi Moore.

➢ The increasing importance of "self-realization" processes.

➢ Reinvention of music, "hip-hop" and "rap," by such groups as "Ice Cube."

➢ A new language form in which English is so mutilated as to be unintelligible. This is being carried over into news readers on prime time television.

These disparate trends signified the emergence of a created climate of social upheaval and far-reaching changes as a new image of human beings began to take hold bringing with them radical changes in Western civilization.

A "leaderless," but powerful network "the invisible army" began working to bring about "unacceptable" change in the United States. Its rank and file members were the "shock troops" who radicalized all forms of the norm, breaking with certain key elements of Western civilization. Among the "Olympians," this network was known as the "Aquarian Conspiracy" and its adherents were to be known as "invisible shock troops."

This massive paradigm gigantic, irrevocable shift, overtook America while we slept, sweeping away the old with new political, religious and philosophical systems. It was what citizens of the New World Order-One World Government would have to exhibit hereafter, a new mind - the rise of a new order with no nation-states, pride of place and pride of race, a culture of the past, destined to the dustbin of history, never to be revived.

We know from experience that this work is likely to be greeted with scorn and disbelief. Some will even pity us. Terms like "off the wall" will be used to describe this work. This is the standard reaction when the motivations of Tavistock's Social scientists brain-washers, opinion-makers, social-psychologists have for acting out their war on the United States are not known. The probability is 90% of the American people do not know that Tavistock declared war on the German civilian population to end WWII.

When that conflict ended in 1946, the Tavistock practitioners of mass brainwashing and opinion went to war against the American people.

If this is how you react when you read this expose, don't feel bad, - then understand that it is the way you are expected to react. If the motivation appears far-fetched and lacking credibility, also incomprehensible, then the motivation "does not exist." That being the case, then the action that derives from it does not exist; therefore, ergo "the Olympians" do not exist and there is no conspiracy.

But the hard fact is that a gigantic conspiracy does exist. No doubt Kurt Lewin, the top scientist at Tavistock and key theoretician of all think tanks could explain it more clearly than we have been able to do, if he chose to. His practice is derived from what he called "topological-psychology" doctrine. Lewin is the man upon whose theories, the psychological warfare battles of World War II were fought so successfully, the man who planned and executed the Strategic Bombing Survey that brought Germany defeat in WWII through the wholesale destruction of 65 percent of German worker housing to which we have just referred to very briefly.

CHAPTER 12

Lewin's doctrine of "identity change"

The Lewin doctrine is not easy for the layman to follow. Basically, Lewin said that all psychological phenomena occur in a domain defined as "psychological phase space." This space is composed of two interdependent "fields," the "environment" and the "self."

The concept of "controlled environment" arose from the study that if you have a fixed-personality (one susceptible to being predictably profiled), and if you want to elicit from this personality a particular type of behavior, then all you have to do is control the third variable of the equation and thus produce the desired behavior.

This was the norm in social-psychology formulas. MI6 uses it, and almost every type of situation involving negotiations; army counterinsurgency operations, labor negotiations and diplomatic negotiations used it up until apparently the 1960s.

After 1960, Tavistock changed the equation by placing greater emphasis on the technique of controlled environment not the behavior, but the desired personality. What Lewin set out to accomplish was far more drastic and permanent; altering the deeper structures of human personalities. In short, what Lewin succeeded in doing was to move beyond "behavior modification" to "identity change."

Identity change was adopted by the nations of the world. Nations worked to acquire a "new personality" that would change the way the world looked at them.

The theory relied upon the original formulations of two Tavistock theoreticians, Dr. William Sargent's theory in his Battle for the Mind, and Kurt Lewin's own work on personality regression.

Lewin observed that the "inner self of the individual displays certain reactions when under tension from the environment. When there is no tension, then the normal inner self of a person is well differentiated, balanced multifaceted, versatile."

"When a reasonable amount of tension is applied from the environment, then all the various abilities and faculties of the inner self go on alert, ready for effective action. But, when an intolerable amount of tension is applied, then this geometry collapses into a blinded, undifferentiated soup; a primitive, a regressed personality. The person is reduced to an animal; the highly differentiated and versatile abilities disappear. The controlled environment takes over the personality."

It is this Lewin "technique" that is used on the captives held at the Guantanamo Bay prison camp in defiance of international law and the U.S. Constitution. The gross misconduct of the Bush administration at the camp is beyond the pale of normal Western Christian civilization, and its acceptance by a docile American public, might be the first sign that the American people have been so changed by Tavistock's "long range penetration and inner-direction conditioning," that they are now ready to descend to the level of the New World Order in a One World Government where such barbaric "treatment" will be regarded as normal and accepted without protest.

The fact that medical doctors took part in the inhuman torture of fellow human being and felt no remorse would indicate just how far down the world has already fallen.

This has been observed as being the basis for the military camp at Guantanamo, Cuba, which was opened there to avoid the strictures of the U.S. Constitution and to provide a Lewin-type controlled environment. The men being held at this psychological prison are now in the state of regression where they have been reduced to the level of animals.

Guantanamo is the type of camp that we predict will be established all over the United States and the world, when the New World Order-One World Government assumes total world control. It is sadistic, inhuman and beastly, designed to break the natural pride of the victims, to break the will to resist and to reduce the prisoners to the level of beasts.

During the first world government experiment in the then USSR, men were allowed to use toilets only to be interrupted in the middle of evacuating and hustled out before they could clean themselves. Abu Graihb and Guantanamo were about at that level when the controllers were roughly subjected to world-wide scrutiny. General Miller who was the chief kapo has since disappeared from sight.

"Dissidents" who insist on the U.S. Government obeying the Constitution and demand their constitutional rights, will in future be treated as "dissidents," exactly like Stalin treated "dissidents" in Russia. Future "Guantanamos" that have sprung up all over America are a portent of the future. On that we can rely.

CHAPTER 13

The Induced Decline of Western Civilization between two World Wars.

Of all European nations, in the period between the two world wars, Germany, as the super-economic, super racial purity, super warrior nation, suffered the most, as was the intention. The League of Nation was the "first draft" of the last- approaching New World Order inside a One World Government, and the "peace proposals" at the Paris Peace Conference, directed and controlled by Tavistock, was meant to cripple Germany and make it a permanent second-class European power, their self-respect destroyed through the social demotion to pauperism or at best proletarian status.

It is hardly surprising that the German people turned savage and gave Hitler the mass following he needed to convert his latent nationalistic movement into a revival force.

We shall never know whether Tavistock miscalculated or indeed, set the stage in this manner for a bigger and bloodier war. After all, Meade and Bertrand Russell had stated, that what was needed was a world populated by "docile" subjects. Russell had remarked on the "child-like" character of the American Negro he had encountered during his travels to the United States. Russell said he preferred them to the white people. He also said that if the White race was to survive, it would have to learn to behave in the child-like manner of the Negro. Yet, in the same breath the Tavistock emissary called black people "useless eaters" and declared that they ought to be wiped out, en-masse.

Russell also liked the docility of the Brazilian people, brought about, he thought, by "inter-race breeding with Africans brought over as slaves."

There is a school of thought that one of the primary objectives of the fiends who planned both world wars was that they would be fought for the most part by young white men. It is certainly true that Germany, Britain, the U.S. and Russia lost millions of the flower of their male population who were removed from the nation-building stock forever. In the Tavistock-engineered WWI, war fronts and battles were arranged in such a manner that Russia lost 9,000,000 men killed or 70 percent of its entire military strength.

With the exception of Russia the aristocracy suffered much less than the bourgeoisie from the economic consequences of war and revolution. Traditionally much of their wealth was in land; which did not depreciate as much during inflation as some tangibles.

The disintegration of the monarchies (except in England) hit the old order of society of the upper-classes, who could not continue to serve society in their roles as officers or diplomats—as there no longer are much demand for their services—opportunities for such service were far fewer than they had been before the war.

Some of the Russia aristocracy courageously accepted proletarian or even menial status like the Russian taxi drivers, night-club doormen, and headwaiters in postwar Paris; others went into business. Most, however, fell into a life of social denigration. Where the strictly guarded frontier between Societies was once impassable in the old monarchic capitals, and cafe society, now appeared large gaps as the lines gradually became blurred.

As the Duke of Windsor put it in his memoirs, A King's Story:

"The force of change had not yet thrust so deeply into the texture of British society as to have obliterated much of the old elegance During the so-called London season the West End was an almost continuous ball from midnight until dawn The evening could always be saved by recourse to one or another of the gay nightclubs, which had then become so fashionable and almost respectable."

(The word "gay" at that time meant "happy". It was not co- opted as a euphemism for sodomy until the mid-fifties.) Nor did the Duke explain that the "force of change" was expertly applied by the Tavistock Institute.

The declining female modesty that became noticeable soon after the end of WWI, suddenly appeared everywhere and with increased velocity. To the uninformed, it was a social phenomenon. Nobody could have suspected that Wellington House and its sinister social engineers were its cause.

Accompanying this testamentary emancipation was a movement of revolt, particularly among young people, against every conventional restraint of mind or body coming to a close amid the shattered idols of the fallen empires. The postwar generation in Europe revolted against every more and custom, as they fought desperately to throw off the horrors of war they had lived through. Necklines plunged, public smoking and drinking became a form of revolt. Homosexuality and lesbianism became demonstrable, not from any inner conviction, but by way of protest at what had happened, and as a rebellion against what the war had destroyed.

Radical and revolutionary excess manifested itself in art, music and fashion. "Jazz" was in the air and "modern art" was thought to be "chic." The comprehensible element in everything was "don't have a care"; it was unsettling and unreal. Those were the years when all of Europe was shell-shocked. Wellington House and Tavistock had done their work well.

Underneath the hectic sense of being propelled forward by uncontrollable events there was a spiritual and emotional numbness. The horror of the war in which millions of young men were needlessly slaughtered, maimed, wounded and gassed was just now beginning to register, so the thing to do was "blot it from remembrances."

The casualties made wars all too real in its ghastly and cruel ugliness, and people recoiled from it in shock and revolution, in the despair brought by disillusionment of peace. Europeans, with their superior culture that epitomized Western civilization were shell-shocked to a greater degree than were Americans.

They lost their faith in the rudiments that made the progress that had sustained their fathers and their grandfathers and made their nations great. And this was particularly true of Germany, Russia, France, and England.

Thinking people could not come to grips with why the world's two most civilized and advanced nations had torn each other to pieces and taken the lives of millions of their finest young manhood. It was as if a terrifying madness had gripped Britain and Germany.

To the initiated it was not madness, but the methodology of Wellington House that gripped the British youth. The fear that it might happen again was what almost prevented the outbreak of WWII.

Officers returning from the carnage described to the news journals the horrors of hand-to-hand combat that had frequently occurred in "the Great War." They were appalled and aghast, horrified and afraid. None of them could understand why there had been a war at all. The dark secrets of Wellington House and the "Olympians" remained hidden, even as they are hidden to this very day.

Where once the laying of a wreath at the Cenotaph in Whitehall, London by the Monarch of England had brought solace, it now engendered bitterness, anger and loathing. The stage was being set for the Second World War in which Tavistock was to play a huge, disproportionate role.

There were the few thinkers who did have something to say: Spengler, in history for example, Hemingway, Evelyn Waugh in literature, and in America Upton Sinclair and Jack London, but their message was also gloomy, even gloomier than Spengler's dark foreboding of the inevitable decline of Western civilization.

It was confirmed by the postwar degradation of personal relationships. Divorce and cheating on one's wife happened more frequently. The beautiful concept of women on a pedestal, women soft and feminine, with a lovely voice filled with cadences, the flower of God's creation, the mystery, was a vanishing ideal. In her place came the strident, the loud, the vulgar with clattering grating speech such as was aped and made popular by a one particular popular morning talk show.

Nobody could possibly know that this sad decline was the end product of Tavistock having declared war on Western womanhood.

In Europe after WWI, the Montparnasse in Paris had become a sad place. Postwar Vienna, emptied by the tide of war that had swept so many of her sons away, was even sadder. But Berlin, once so bustling and so clean, became the Babylon of Europe and perhaps the saddest place of them all.

"Whoever lived through these apocalyptic month, these years, became disgusted and embittered, sensed the coming of a counter-blow, a horrible reaction," wrote the historian, Zweig.

The political, spiritual, and social bankruptcy of the new power elites, who succeeded the monarchs, the aristocrats and the old-fashioned bourgeois dynasties, was in many respects more spectacular than that of their predecessors, and nowhere more so than in the United States, with the coming of the Socialist era under Franklin D. Roosevelt. This time, however, the eclipse of leadership was not localized in one continent or limited to any particular class of society.

The geographical New World, in terms of the problems that confronted it, the America of Franklin Roosevelt soon demonstrated that the United States was scarcely less anachronistic than the Austria-Hungary of Franz Joseph had been. Here he was establishing a "Democratic" New World Order Socialism straight out of the model created by the Fabian Society, while the United States was a confederated constitutional Republic, the exact opposite.

Neither the shift of the European locus of power and prestige from the former Central Empire Western democracies, nor the replacement of the traditional ruling classes within the fallen monarchies to the United States, did anything to the improve economic, political, social, moral or religious climate of the post WWI world. The Wall Street Crash and the Depression that followed, bear eloquent, if silent witness to the truth and accuracy of our statement.

The manner in which this event was contrived by the Tavistock Institute can be seen in the timetable of events that which we provide in the Appendix.

CHAPTER 14

America is not a "Homeland"

The United States of America has long been the most fertile ground for the wholesale spread of propaganda, its people having been connived, lied to, cheated, at which the British have always led the world, the premiere mind control- brainwashing and propaganda center in the world being the Tavistock Institute of Human Relations. Its forerunner was the organization put together by Lord Northcliffe, who married into the Rothschild family, and who was ably assisted by Lord Rothmere and the Americans, Walter Lippman and Edward Bernays.

From this modest beginning in 1914 grew the Tavistock Institute of Human Relations, which has no peer when it came to creating propaganda. Tavistock is a facility dedicated to the propagation of propaganda to suit every aspect of life. Tavistock approached propaganda as if it were going into battle, and in a sense, it was. There are no half- measures; it was a war where anything goes as long as it assures victory.

Surveying the political scene one cannot escape the fact that in the past two decades, the increase in depth and volume of propaganda, and more especially, mind control, has become all pervasive. The correct application of propaganda to any theme, whether it is economic, or political, is an essential element in the control-mechanism of government.

Stalin once said that if one wanted a docile population then fear and terror had to be unleashed against them. In a sense that is what happened in the United States and Britain.

The Second World War provided unlimited opportunities of developing propaganda into a fine art. Looking back on the efforts made by the Roosevelt administration to cause the American people — who were 87 percent against going to war in Europe change their minds, we find that in spite of everything, Roosevelt did not succeed. The American people rejected entry into the war in Europe.

It took a contrived situation, a contrived pre-chosen pretext, the Japanese attack on Pearl Harbor, to reverse public opinion in favor of America's entry into the European war. Roosevelt held out that America was fighting for democracy and its very way of life, neither of which bore the slightest resemblance to the truth; the war was fought to advance the cause of International Socialism toward its goal of a New World Order inside a One World Government.

Propaganda, to be successful, must be aimed at the total population and not at individuals or individual groups, the purpose being to attract the widest possible attention. It is not intended as personal instruction. Facts play no role in propaganda which is always to create an impression. It has to one-sided systematic, sustained indoctrination that what the Government, the media and political leaders are saying is the truth. And it has to be pitched in such a manner that the people feel that it is their thinking.

Thus, propaganda has to be directed at mass audiences where its message will make its mark. Let us take a recent example of the type of propaganda that would usually be embraced by a receptive audience. In the wake of the World Trade Center disaster, President Bush created a new Government agency, which he called the Office of Homeland Security, and appointed a director to oversee the agency.

Now this sounds very comforting and very soothing until we look at the 10th Amendment, which reserves all such powers as Mr.

Bush proposed to seize, to the several States.

The fact that Mr. Bush cannot overrule the 10th Amendment was blithely ignored. The propaganda blurb says he can, and since it was directed to the masses, they believed the blurb, rather than their Constitution, and so there was little effective opposition to this gross violation of the Constitution, particularly the 10th Amendment. Bush appears to have been operating under the Stalin directive: "If you want to control the people, first terrorize them."

Those who opposed the "Homeland Security" quasi-law, were dubbed, "unpatriotic" and "favoring terrorism." Again, the absolute fact that this bogus act is no law at all and is sheer propaganda was never called into question, but was accepted by the "rah-rah" unthinking public. Public opinion is made in this way and public opinion is what swayed legislators to vote for "Homeland Security" or any other bogus laws, as Bernays and Lippmann both asserted in the very early days of Wellington House. The legislators vote along party lines as in the British Parliamentary system, and do not vote on the basis of the U.S. Constitution. They knew that to oppose the President, they stand a good chance of losing a cozy job at the next election, or face being smeared by some sleazy muck-racking "administration" man.

America is not one "homeland" but 50 distinct and separate States. In any case the word "homeland" comes straight out of the Communist Manifesto. Since the ultimate goal of government is to establish a New World Order International Communist One World Government, the choice of this word to title Communist legislation, should not surprise us.

The power to control Education, Welfare and Police Powers belongs to the States where it has always resided, and it was not taken away from the States at the time of the covenant. Neither President Bush nor the House and Senate have any power to change that, which the newly created office proposed to do. It was only through the exercise of sustained, systematic, repetition of propaganda that the people of the States accepted this gross violation of the U.S. Constitution.

The drumbeat of propaganda continued through numerous articles about the background and experience of the "Homeland Director" and what his job is etc., but there is not one word about the blatant unconstitutionality of the new department. It will not escape your notice that the very title: "Homeland Security" is a clever little bit of propaganda. The people are now convinced that not only is the new agency constitutional, but that it is also necessary. The mass of people has now been successfully "mind controlled" (brainwashed.)

Those who wish to study the matter instead of merely watching the CBS Evening News will find something quite different from an account of an independent commentator and the accounts in the press. As always, such person will be in the minority, so that his opinions, even if expressed, will not alter the purpose and intent of setting up the new agency. I say to you that the United States is forbidden by its Constitution and the constitutions of the separate 50 States from having any central Federal control mechanism imposed upon them. The so-called "Homeland Security" bill is a travesty, because it destroys the Republican form of government granted to the original states in the 10th Amendment, and which cannot be taken away from them.

The so-called "Homeland Security Act" is therefore, null and void and no law at all. Yet, the brainwashed inner-directed victims of Tavistock will obey it as if it were law.

In short the Homeland Security agency is a deception and it cannot be made law. No measure that is unconstitutional can be enacted into law and the Congress has urgent duty repeal the "law" that gave illegitimate birth to the "Homeland" and "Patriot" Acts forthwith. The cardinal point to remember is that propaganda and mass brainwashing must always be viewed in relation to the end it is intended to serve. In this instance it convinces the populace, that liberties must be sacrificed in exchange for "protection." Henry Clay, the greatest constitutional scholar who ever lived called the ploy "a doctrine of necessity, a doctrine from Hell" and utterly condemned such attempts.

H. V. Dicks taught at Tavistock. He stated that individual rights have to be sacrificed for the good of all! That includes the measure violating the highest law of the land! It must be accepted because it is for the good of all! This is better explained if we take as an example, the propaganda and brainwashing that accompanied President Roosevelt's desperate efforts to involve the United States in the war going on in Europe, via Japan.

When the anticipated attack on Pearl Harbor happened, (Roosevelt knew the day and the time it would take place) announced in his speeches written for him by the Tavistock Institute, that the American people would be fighting for the highest and noblest of causes, the defense of the nation, defense of freedom and for the future security and well-being of the nation. As is usual in such cases, the facts spoke of a far different set of objectives.

Roosevelt did not say that the American people were going to war to fight for the advancement of International Socialism and for the goals of the New World Order -International Communism, One World Government.

The American people were told that Germany intended to enslave the world. This was a very good line because even the most poorly educated of people realize that slavery is one of the worst fates that mankind could be called on to suffer. By introducing the word "slavery" a sympathetic chord was struck.

Once again, propaganda bore no relationship to the facts.

Thinking persons, not susceptible to propaganda, would have realized that a small nation like Germany could not possibly enslave the world even if had wanted to do so. The resources and manpower were just not there. Germany did not possess the vast maritime fleet to make such an attack on the United States a real possibility.

The promoters of the war realized from the very outset that for momentum to be maintained, a sustained blast of propaganda would be necessary. The same principle was followed by Vice President Cheney in the weeks preceding the U.S. attack on Iraq; he distorted facts, delivered blast after blast of "fear rhetoric" and twisted intelligence information to fit his purposes. Nobody worked harder than Cheney to ensure that war with Iraq would not be prevented at the last minute.

It was important that Roosevelt attract the attention of the masses the "issues" and bring them home to the people, hence the endless press reports, the "newsreels" shown endlessly at cinemas and the endless brainwashing speeches of the politicians.

Propaganda has to be in a medium easily understood by the lowest level of intelligence among the nation, such as posters depicting workers in munitions factories, shipyards; aircraft-assembly plants all working on the "home front" for the "war effort" and so on.

In the aftermath of the WTC tragedy, much of that type of mass-brainwashing propaganda was revived: "America at War", "the front line", "and munitions dumps", "enemy troop positions" appeared as sub headings on almost everything televisions screened.

The fact that the United States was not at war because war had not been declared, and that there were no enemy "troops" other than loosely knit guerilla groups, was of course omitted.

Dictionaries define troops as "a body of soldiers; an army, generally in the plural." The Taliban had no army, and therefore, no troops. Besides which, war could not be declared on "terrorism" or "Bolshevism" or any other "ism." War can only be declared against sovereign nations, this according to the U.S. Constitution.

War can only be declared on a country or a particular nation of people inhabiting that country. Anything else is Tavistock balderdash dished up on a platter decorated with waving flags and to the accompaniment of martial music. To say that that the United States is at war with the Taliban is the height of deception. To be at war of necessity demands a prior declaration of war. Without a declaration of war it is deception, in effect no war at all.

A new dimension was added. President Bush, denied war-making powers and law- making powers by the U.S. Constitution, was suddenly imbued with powers, which didn't exist in the U.S. Constitution.

He began to be called "the commander in chief," when he was not entitled to the temporary title, which can only be conferred by the Congress in the wake of a full declaration of war. That never happened.

He was mystically "declared" as having the power to label any person he so chose an "enemy combatant." That there is no such empowerment in the U.S. Constitution, nor is it expressly implied, did not faze Mr. Bush for a moment: As far as he was concerned from then on, he was the law.

Thus, the illicit, unconstitutional seizure of powers by a sitting U.S. President that began with Woodrow Wilson "taking" ten additional powers to which he was absolutely not entitled, expanded with Roosevelt "taking" thirty and H. V. Bush taking thirty-five (and counting) powers denied by the U.S.

Constitution.

Indeed, the United States has become a lawless nation under the expert guidance of the Tavistock Institute whose "inner-directional conditioning and long-range penetration" brainwashing of the American public made it all possible.

In passing let me add that the British propaganda establishment used the self-same language of lies against the Boers in South Africa in the war launched by the British to take control of the massive gold deposits in that land. The British press was full of accounts of the "Boer Army" when the Boers had no army, only a farmer citizen guerilla force.

Like Kaiser Wilhelm II in 1913/1914, Paul Kruger, the God-fearing patriarch of the Transvaal Republic was demonized in the British press as a vicious tyrant who brutally repressed the black population, none of which bore the slightest resemblance to the truth.

Eventually, a formula was arrived at through a series of trials and errors in WWI and WWII, and it was revived and adapted for use in the U.S. attack on Afghanistan. It was enough to catch the fancy and the attention of the bulk of the American population because it was pitched to their psychological level. The lessons learned in the art of propaganda in the two World Wars were simply switched from the European theater to mainstream USA, and later, to Iraq, Serbia and Afghanistan.

The brainwashing was kept strictly to bare essentials, embodied in simplistic slogans, catch-phrases using stereotyped formulas first developed by Lord Northcliffe at Wellington House in London in 1912. The British people had to be educated that the German people were "the enemy." Everything evil and cruel was imputed all things German, so that the mass of British people began to believe that the Germans actually were cruel barbarians who would stop at nothing. Posters depicting the "Boche butchers" killing Belgian women and children sprang up all over the place.

CHAPTER 15

The Media's role in propaganda

As the media played a huge role in propaganda, it is perhaps a good idea to see where this started and how it has come to pass that the media in the U.S. almost in its entirety is now a fully controlled, propaganda organ. The period prior to the First World War was a classic series of events in which personalities were manipulated, the worst offenders being the British and American newspapers. As in all wars, someone has to be demonized to get the public involved. In 1913 it was Kaiser Wilhelm II of Germany who was demonized before, during and after that terrible war.

One of the principle creators of propaganda of that period was Lord Nortcliffe, the noted press baron, a relative of the Rothschilds and a hater of Germany. Northcliffe ran Wellington House as a major center for anti-German propaganda and he harbored a particular hatred of Wilhelm II, who was a cousin of Queen Victoria of the notorious Black Guelph dynasty of Venice.

Northcliffe abused Wilhelm II on every possible occasion especially on the occasions when the Kaiser talked about Germany's military might and prowess. Wilhelm was given to childish boasting and most European governments knew him as a man who liked to "play soldiers", and dressing in outlandishly decorated uniforms. Wilhelm was very distinctly not a military man. As a Rothschild, this irked Northcliffe who began "warning" that "Germany's place in the sun" as the Kaiser liked to call it, was a danger to the rest of Europe. That this claim was without the slightest foundation did not seem to bother

Northcliffe who maximized it to the extent where it was marvelous to behold.

The truth is that Germany was not a threat at that time and nor was the Kaiser a mighty warrior waiting to strike, but rather, a man prone to nervous breakdowns of which he had three in five years and a near useless withered arm, which did not project a martial man at all. The nearest one can say that Wilhelm got to being martial, was his love of dressing up in extravagantly bedecked uniforms. In truth Wilhelm II had little if any control over the German military, a fact that Northcliffe was well aware of and yet chose to ignore.

In this the Kaiser was on the same level as the British monarch, King George V who had no control of the British Expeditionary Force. That didn't stop Northcliffe of launching a blistering attack on Queen Victoria's German cousin, blaming him for being responsible for a whole list of atrocities allegedly carried out by the German Army driving through Belgium. Of course, the German High Command did wrong in invading neutral Belgium, but they were only in transit with no plans to occupy the country.

It was all part of a tactical plan to march on Paris taking a "short cut" through Belgium to outflank the French Army. There would have been nothing to gain by deliberately killing civilians, a fact the German High Command has stressed. Northcliffe called the Kaiser a "megalomaniac" with a "hunger to rule the world" which in any case was quite beyond the capabilities of any European power. In 1940 Churchill accused Hitler of having the same desire to 'rule the world" knowing it to be false. Churchill also declared Hitler "a madman" knowing his characterization of the chancellor to be false.

But not to be discouraged, Northcliffe had his media outlets constantly refer to Wilhelm II as "the mad dog of Europe."

Wellington House engaged the services of a cartoonist who regularly depicted Wilhelm II as a slavering mad dog, an ape-like creature. The cheap cartoons were made up into book form, and quickly granted a status by the press that was absolute nonsense. The cartoons were in poor taste and even poorer execution. The book was what the English used to call "a penny horrible."

Showing the power of the press, Northcliffe got the media to give rave revues about the book. Lord Asquith, the Prime Minister, was persuaded to write a forward to what was essentially an absolute farce. President Wilson invited the "artist," a Dutchman by the name of Raemakers, to the White House when he was on a book-selling tour of the U.S. As was expected, Wilson lionized the cartoonist and gave his blessing to the book.

Even the legendary "Punch" magazine joined in the campaign to depict Wilhelm in the most unfavorable light. It seemed that no journal escaped having to print the torrent of sewage that poured forth from Wellington House. It was propaganda in its rawest form.

It was not long thereafter that the effect rubbed off on the people who began insisting that the Kaiser "be hanged" and one minister of religion went as far as to say that he would forgive Germany as long as all Germans were shot. Hollywood soon joined in the act of condemning the Kaiser, of whom it knew nothing. First off was the movie My Four Years in Germany adapted from a book written by U.S. ambassador to Berlin, James W. Gerard. The movie was depicted as a factual account of the Kaiser preparing for war. Wilhelm was given the IQ of a paranoid six-year old child and depicted as a man riding a hobbyhorse. Scathing descriptions of his disability were repeated hundreds of times.

Worse was tc come with the Hollywood version of history entitled The Beast of Berlin that portrayed the Kaiser gloating over slaughtered Belgian civilians and chuckling in mirth over torpedoed ships. None of which was true, but it served its purpose, generating a fierce hate against Germans and all things German that spread across the U.S. with astonishing rapidity.

It was the basis of the worst type of propaganda ever seen and it was carried out in a relentless fashion by the British Government, not only at home, but also where it counted the most, in the United States. Wellington House was counting on the United States to defeat Germany on the field of battle.

In the late 1990's it was but a very short step for the mass of the American people to believe the same of the Taliban and of President Hussein of Iraq with who the Taliban was not connected. (In fact they hated each other.)

The fundamental question: "Were the Taliban as a whole, and the people of Afghanistan, separate from the Taliban, responsible for the dastardly bombing of the WTC?" Does the Taliban actually exist? Or is Osama bin Laden just another Kaiser Wilhelm II? Perhaps, fifty years hence we might find out the truth. In the meantime the Tavistock Institute played the propaganda card to the limit, and once again, it succeeded.

After the end of the war the myth of Kaiser Wilhelm II persisted. In fact the same propaganda machine that had demonized him before and during the war, did not give way until July 13, 1959, the 100th anniversary of Kaiser Wilhelm II birthday, which was celebrated by the BBC in the form of a documentary about the much abused former German leader.

It explained how the British people were terrorized by bloodcurdling accounts of the Kaiser slashing arms off Belgian children with his sword while columns of German soldiers raped women in the Belgian villages they passed through, none of the accounts bearing even a faint resemblance to the truth.

Even intelligent members of the British Parliament were taken in by the relentless storm of hatred stirred up by Northcliffe and his crew that included the Americans Lippmann and Bernays. However, as good as it was, the BBC documentary made no effort to explain how the myth of a monstrous Kaiser Wilhelm could suddenly arise as if from nowhere, to take up the headlines in the newspapers?

In the same way no one has explained to my satisfaction how Osama bin Laden suddenly appeared on the scene, and how he became the villain in the manner of the Kaiser in an amazingly short period of time. How did this happen?

It is an historical fact, that President Wilson rushed the bill to establish the Federal Reserve banks to the House, just in time for the start of WWI period. Without paper dollars, printed at will, it is doubtful, that the war would have occurred.

How could the Kaiser have suddenly come alive from the cartoon character staring out of thousands of newspapers, magazines and billboards? We know now that he was the product of the vast British War Office's propaganda machine, which remained secret as it still remains a big secret organization to this very day. The machinery remains as covert today as it was in 1913, although some of us have managed to tear away some of its shrouding.

One thing we unearthed through research is that the Tavistock Institute was the birthplace of some of the most preposterous lies ever to be manufactured and held up as truth.

CHAPTER 16

Scientific propaganda can deceive the very elect.

The vast majority of people in the world today will surely have heard of the "Beast of Berlin" and how the "Allies" put to an end to his mad rampage through Europe. Most people in recent times have also heard of the "Beast of Baghdad."

But how many have heard of the name, Sir Harold Nicholson, a distinguished scholar, whose thorough examination of literally hundreds of thousands of documents from 1912 to 1925, absolutely exonerated Kaiser Wilhelm II from starting WWI?

How many people know this? Put it to the test. Try your local talk show whiz, and see what happens. Thus for more than twenty five years the myth of the Kaiser dominated the headlines and had the effect of turning millions of people in Britain and America, against Germany in an unjust and unfortunate by product of the vast propaganda machine that has the British people by the throat since it was first opened for business in 1913. We speak of Wellington House and its successor, the Tavistock Institute for Human Relations.

The amazing thing about the myth is how long it lasted. But the purpose of propaganda is precisely to perpetuate a myth, a lie or some piece of misinformation that lives long after the truth is forgotten. Japan will forever be blamed for Pearl Harbor, and for the "rape of Nanking," while Churchill will forever be hailed as a great man, instead of a brutal warmonger.

In the same way Colin Powell recently visited Iraq and came out with a banner headline statement about Hussein "gassing Kurds" during the Iraq-Iran war.

The truth is that the gas-filled missiles that fell on the Kurdish village were Phosgene, a type not possessed by Iraq, but they were in the arsenal of Iran. What happened was that during an Iraqi offensive, the Iranians fired a large number of gas-filled rockets at Iraqi position, but some fell short among the Kurds along the border. This was confirmed by the U.S. Military College of War report, which entirely exonerated Iraq.

Yet, although the accusation was thoroughly refuted, in 2005, almost 30 years later, while on a goodwill tour of Malaysia, Karen Hughes representing President George Bush repeated the lie, embellishing it by claiming that "30,000 Kurds" had been gassed to death by "Saddam Hussein." A member of the audience contested her statement, and the next day Hughes was forced to retract her story, saying that she had "misspoken" herself. An investigation into the incident revealed that Hughes actually believed the lies she had heard repeated over and over again, by President Bush, Prime Minister Blair, Secretary of States Colin Powell, and Secretary of Defense Donald Rumsfeld, which ought to tell us a great deal about the power of propaganda.

The facts of the case reported by the War College were later confirmed by the U.S. Army and by a second U.S. source. Does the world know this? We doubt it. Truth is forgotten while a lie lives on. Thus Colin Powell's propaganda against Iraq will go the way of the propaganda against Kaiser Wilhelm II, on and on for more than 100 years, while the truth died the moment the first propaganda blast appeared in the newspapers. In this lies the value of propaganda. The Social scientists at Tavistock know this and today, they can profile any audience to accept lies best suited to their perception without understanding the issues behind it.

By this manner a "morally correct" position and a solid backing for the attack on Afghanistan was created. Few of the American people ever raised doubts about whether what their government was doing in Afghanistan was in accordance with the U.S. Constitution. There was no referendum, and no mandate to confirm or deny acceptance by the people of the Bush administration's policy toward Afghanistan.

Propaganda-brainwashing does not call for a mandate. The fact that none of the alleged hijackers of the planes used against the Twin Towers were from Afghanistan was completely lost on the American public, 74 percent of whom still believe that the "al Qaeda" did it and that they live in Afghanistan! The same percentage of Americans were brainwashed to believe that the Taliban and President Hussein worked together to bring about the tragedy! The American people do not know that Saddam Hussein would have nothing to do with the Taliban leadership.

Why do the American people allow themselves to be treated in this manner? Why do they allow politicians to lie, cheat, connive, dissemble, prevaricate, obfuscate and continually deceive them? What we ought to mark well, is the way Woodrow Wilson treated the American people, like sheep.

When asked why he kept a small flock of sheep grazing on the White House lawns, Wilson replied: "They remind me of the American people." Wilson had a burning ambition to rush America into WWI and he used Wellington House lies (propaganda) against dissenters (the bulk of the people) to persuade them to change their outlook.

Roosevelt repeated the ploy to get the U.S. into WWII through lies and propaganda (most often than not the same thing) culminating in the "success" of Pearl Harbor. We saw the same line used by Pres. Clinton. In the run-up to and during the unjust war against Serbia, Clinton's entire persuasion consisted of lies and disinformation, not to mention misinformation.

No wonder that Rumsfeld pronouncements are always met with suspicion. When asked about the role being played by propaganda, Rumsfeld blandly replied: "Government officials, the Department of Defense, this secretary of defense and the people who work with me tell the American people the truth."

CHAPTER 17

Propaganda and Psychological Warfare

A list of U.S. Government Papers, some available and some not, reveal in a striking manner just how controlled the nations of the world (including the United States) have become due to the exercise of propaganda methods at an astonishing array of levels.

At best, I can only mention the titles and paraphrase content because of the vastness of the material. I hope the information we have put together will shock the American people out of their slumbering apathy and make them realize just how far they are on the road to becoming slaves of the Socialist New World Order inside a One World Government.

Official Definitions: A useful collection of terms and definitions as used by the Washington power establishment. Without exception every single one of the programs cited herein are Tavistock born and bred.

Social Sciences and Political Intervention: What passes itself off as project-centered "development assistance" may in reality consist of dangerous manipulation of culture and social relations in the southern hemisphere.

Because of the enormous monetary advantage enjoyed by donors of "aid," they are often in a position to do extensive psychosocial studies of target groups and to exploit them in ways that would not occur to most people, even in their worst nightmares.

It is typical of everything John Rawlings Reese taught at

Tavistock and it was carried into every aspect of American life Shock and Awe: Achieving Rapid Dominance - This is the National Defense University text (1996) that became the theory behind U.S. intervention in the Middle East and the war against Iraq in March and April of 2003. "Shock and Awe," says the text, is intended to be the "non-nuclear equivalent" of the bombing of Hiroshima and Nagasaki in 1945.

Says the now out-of-print study guide of that terrible tragedy says: "The impact of those weapons was sufficient to transform both the mindset of the average Japanese citizen and the outlook of the leadership through this condition of Shock and Awe. The Japanese simply could not comprehend the destructive power carried by a single airplane. This incomprehension produced a state of awe."

Besides using massive firepower for psychological purposes, the publication also includes extensive discussion of propaganda operations. "The principal mechanism for achieving this dominance is through imposing sufficient conditions of "Shock and Awe" on the adversary to convince or compel it to accept our strategic aims and military objectives," the writers state. "Clearly, deception, confusion, misinformation, and disinformation, perhaps in massive amounts, must be employed."

Psychological Warfare in Combat: This is the full text of the infamous "Shock and Awe" doctrine, published in 1996 by the National Defense University, Washington. The concept is to gain complete control over the will of an adversary, as well as the perceptions and understanding of target peoples, literally making an enemy impotent to act or react.

It is worth noting that all of these words and descriptions were found in text books used to condition students attending classes conducted by John Rawlings Reese at the British Army Psychological Warfare Bureau where Rawlings was a master theoretician.

The "Shock & Awe" doctrine is described as a strategy to achieve the systematic destruction of military capability through attrition, where appropriate, and to use overwhelming force to paralyze shock, unnerve, and ultimately accomplish the moral destruction of an opponent.

The International Conference on Population and Development (ICPD): A Program of Action presented at the conference called for massive propaganda effort, utilizing the mass media, non-governmental organizations, commercial entertainment, and academic institutions in an effort to "persuade" people in developing countries to change their fertility preferences.

A revision to the original text added to accommodate representatives from developing countries urges that communications activities carried out by donors "for advocacy purposes or to promote particular lifestyles" should be labeled in such a way that the public will be aware of their purpose and that "the identity of sponsors should be indicated in an appropriate manner."

Despite this recommendation, which imposes no mandatory restrictions on aid donors, the "communication" section of document remains a very dangerous and politically explosive part of the New World Order agenda.

The Population Communication Project: The U.S. Agency for International Development (USAID) has poured tens of millions of dollars into a "mass media" influence campaign that uses tactics borrowed from military psychological-war operatives. USAID is only one of hundreds of U.S. Government agencies that contracted with Tavistock to write its programs.

In fact, the contractor working as a proxy for USAID in this case was also under contract to the U.S. Army to prepare teaching manuals for psychological operations.

Enter-Educate: Using Entertainment as Propaganda: The young audience is likely to be more vulnerable to messages presented in the context of "entertainment" than to other communications that might tend to raise questions about the legitimacy of foreign ideas.

Thus, the entertainment-propaganda approach has become a huge part of USAID's international population control effort. Here again, literary millions of dollars has gone to Tavistock for programs taught by Enter-Educate operators.

When Propaganda Backfires: A study done of family planning attitudes and behavior done in the north of Nigeria in 1994. According to a published report, the negative reaction illustrated "opposition to outsider improprieties, to family planning in general and to U.S.-sponsored family planning programs in particular."

Nigeria Bilateral Population Program: (U.S. State Department document). The major planning document of the U.S. government's population control strategy for Nigeria.

It is also used as an important part of propaganda in Psychological Warfare employed in the U.S. Government programs to undermine Latin American political movements, the anti-war effort, movement, and grassroots political organizing. The contract to write this program was awarded to Tavistock.

Post-Modern Warfare: A menu of resources about political/psychological warfare, covert activities, and genocide.

Urban De-Concentration and Other Tactics: This is so diabolical in content that I do not propose publishing it at least for now.

Social Influence: Propaganda and Persuasion: — Some useful background information.

Psychological Operations in Guerrilla Warfare: The CIA's tactical manual for paramilitary forces in Central America prepared by Tavistock. The CIA has Tavistock under contract and works very closely with it.

Institute for Propaganda Analysis: A collection of documents containing basic facts about covert influence campaigns. Here again, the institute is merely a clearing house for Tavistock data and brainwashing methods for mass use.

The United States Intelligence Bureaus Official descriptions and duties of U.S. government bureaus involved in the collection or analysis of intelligence.

Secrecy & Government Bulletins: A collection of documents advocating openness in government.

Reporters Collective: A source for reliable research materials on international institutions and their role in fronting for the wealthy, powerful nations that control their policies. Many of the institutions listed have had their leadership cadre taught by Tavistock's Social Science scientists.

Propaganda, dissemination of ideas and information for the purpose of inducing or intensifying specific attitudes and actions: Because propaganda is frequently accompanied by distortions of fact and by appeals to passion and prejudice, it is often thought to be invariably false or misleading. As Tavistock's manuals state, the essential distinction lies in the intentions of the propagandist to persuade an audience to adopt the attitude or action he or she espouses. Wilson and Roosevelt were examples of this truism, both having been polished in the art of diplomacy by deception as Bukanin explained the term back in 1814.

CHAPTER 18

Wilson gets the U.S. into WWI thanks to propaganda

The massive modern propaganda techniques which have become a familiar part of particularly the American and British governments began with World War I (1914-1918). From the beginning of the war, both German and British propagandists worked hard to win sympathy and support of the United States. German propagandists appealed to the many Americans of German descent, and to those of Irish descent, who were traditionally hostile to Great Britain who was living in America. The propaganda was rather crude by today's standards, but what it lacked in finesse was made up by the sheer volume of the huge output of Wellington House.

Soon, however, Germany was virtually cut off from direct access to the United States. Thereafter British propaganda had little competition in the United States, and it was conducted more skillfully than that of the Germans who had no equivalent of Wellington House, Bernays, or Lippmann.

Once engaged in the war Woodrow Wilson organized the Committee on Public Information, an official propaganda agency, to mobilize American public opinion. This committee proved highly successful, particularly in the sale of Liberty Bonds. And no wonder. Its program was written for the White House by Tavistock and was largely directed from London.

The exploitation by the Allies of President Woodrow Wilson's Fourteen Points, which seemed to promise a just peace for both the victors and the vanquished, contributed greatly toward crystallizing opposition within the Central Powers to continuation of the war.

Elsewhere herein we have detailed the lies and distortions engaged in by the Bryce Commission, which remains one of the most disturbing examples of blatant lying successfully passed off as truth. The part played by Americans at Wellington House, the premiere propaganda center in the world at that time is also explained later herein.

The propaganda aspects of World War II were similar to those of World War I, except that the Second World War, also started by Britain and financed by the international bankers, was greater in scope. Radio played a major role, with "news broadcasts" always a mixture of facts heavily laced with fiction. Propaganda activities overseas were more intense. The Tavistock Institute was able to put into practice all of the valuable lessons it had learned in 1914-1919, and it used its experience in a number of new ways in the old as well as new countries.

Both Germany and the United Kingdom again sought to sway American opinion. German propagandists played on anti- British sentiment, represented the war as a struggle against communism, and pictured Germany as the invincible champion of a new wave of anti-Communism. German agents also gave their support to movements in the United States that backed "isolationism", a descriptive tag attached to all Americans who opposed war with Germany.

German propaganda efforts were no match against the expertise of Wellington House and Tavistock or the resources of Britain (secretly aided with huge amounts of money by the Roosevelt administration) and once again it proved ineffective.

The carefully planned attack on Pearl Harbor was well known by Roosevelt, Stimson and Knox for months before the actual attack.

December 1941, was a godsend for Roosevelt who had been trying desperately to force the U.S. to go to war on the side of Britain, especially after the Japanese attack on Pearl Harbor; American people were persuaded by propaganda and outright lies that Germany was the aggressor.

The dire warnings by Lindbergh, the famous aviator, and a number of other anti-war Senators that Roosevelt was not to be trusted, and that as was the case in WWI, the U.S. had no business interjecting itself into the war in Germany, was blunted by propaganda. Also, the "contrived situation" at Pearl Harbor changed public opinion, as Roosevelt well knew it would. Allied propaganda efforts that flowed from Tavistock were aimed at separating the peoples of the Axis nations from their governments, which were held solely to blame for the war. Radio broadcasts and leaflets dropped from the air carried Allied propaganda to the enemy.

The official U.S. propaganda agencies during World War II were the Office of War Information (OWI), charged with disseminating Tavistock "information" at home and abroad, and the Office of Strategic Service (OSS), forerunner of the CIA and a creation of Tavistock, charged with conducting psychological warfare against the enemy.

At Supreme Headquarters in the European theater of operations, the OWI and OSS were coordinated with military activities by the Psychological Warfare Division under the direction of Social scientists from the Tavistock Institute.

In the period of the Cold War—a marked conflict of interests between the United States and the Soviet Union following World War II—propaganda continued to be a significant instrument of national policy.

Both the democratic and Communist blocs of states attempted by sustained campaigns, to win to their side the great masses of uncommitted peoples, and thereby, achieve their objectives, without resorting to armed conflict. Every aspect of national life and policy was exploited for purposes of propaganda.

The Cold War was also marked by the use of defectors, trials, and confessions for propaganda purposes. In this propaganda war the Communist nations seemed initially to have a distinct advantage. Because their governments controlled all media, they could largely seal off their people from Western propaganda.

At the same time, the highly centralized governments could plan elaborate propaganda campaigns and mobilize resources to carry out their plans. They could also count on aid from Communist parties and sympathizers in other countries. Democratic states, on the other hand, could neither prevent their peoples from being exposed to Communist propaganda nor mobilize all their resources to counter it. This apparent advantage for Communist governments eroded during the 1980s, as communications technology advanced. Inability to control the spread of information was a major factor in the disintegration of many Communist regimes in Eastern Europe at the end of the decade. The United States Information Agency (USIA), established in 1953 to conduct propaganda and cultural activities abroad, operates the "Voice of America", a radio network that carries news and information about the United States in more than 40 languages to all parts of the world.

CHAPTER 19

Is history being repeated? The case of Lord Bryce

With historians heavily involved in either defending or damning the war in Iraq, it might be good time to ponder the case of Viscount James Bryce, the highly respected historian who sold out and went to his grave as a confirmed, dastardly, unrepentant liar. Before his unfortunate involvement with Wellington House, Bryce had enjoyed wide respect as an honest historian.

From the start of World War I, stories of German atrocities filled British and American newspapers. By far the bulk of them were prepared at Wellington House and spread through media channels. Mostly, they were supposed to have emanated from "eye-witness" accounts by "reporters and photographers," who accompanied the German Army's march through Belgium to outflank French defenses in their drive on Paris.

Eyewitnesses described German infantrymen spearing Belgian babies on their bayonets as they marched along, singing war songs. Accounts of Belgian boys and girls with amputated hands (supposedly to prevent them from using guns) abounded. Tales of women with amputated breasts multiplied even faster.

At the top of the atrocity hit parade were rape stories. One eyewitness claimed the Germans dragged twenty young women out of their houses in a captured Belgian town and stretched them on tables in the village square, where each was violated by at least twelve "Huns," while the rest of the division watched and cheered. At British expense, a group of Belgians toured the

United States retelling these stories.

President Woodrow Wilson solemnly received them in the White House. Their story horrified America. Nobody thought to check their account of the rape they had witnessed. Their accounts of the brutality they allegedly had suffered were never questioned.

The Germans angrily denied these stories. So did American reporters with the German army. In 1914 Wilson had not yet "managed" the battlefield reporters unlike George Bush in the invasion of Iraq in 2002. There were no "embedded" reporters with the British Army. Tavistock had yet to learn how to censor the truth by "embedding" selected reporters with the troops.

When British journalist's dispatches began to be published in England, throwing doubt of the "atrocities", Northcliffe came up with the idea of appointing Lord Bryce to head an enquiry board to investigate accounts of German atrocities and report back to him. Actually the suggestion came from Edward Bernays and was approved by Walter Lippmann.

Then, early in 1915, the British government made it official by asking Viscount Bryce to head a royal commission to investigate the atrocity reports. Bryce was one of the best- known historians of the era; he had written widely praised books on the American government and on Irish history, sympathetically portraying the Irish people's hard fate under British rule. In 1907, he had worked with an Anglo-Irish diplomat, Roger Casement, to expose horrendous exploitation of Indian peoples on the Amazon River by a British rubber company.

From 1907-1913, he had served as British ambassador in Washington, where he became a popular, even beloved figure.

It would have been hard to find a more admired scholar who had an established reputation of honesty and integrity. Bryce and his six fellow commissioners, an amalgam of distinguished lawyers, historians land jurists, "analyzed" 1,200 depositions of "eyewitnesses," who claimed to have seen all manner of atrocious German behavior.

Almost all the testimony came from Belgians who had fled to England as refugees; and there were some statements from Belgian and British soldiers, collected in France. But the commissioners failed to interrogate even a single one of these eyewitnesses; that task was left to "gentlemen of legal knowledge and experience"—lawyers. Since the asserted crimes took place in what continued to be a war zone, there was no on site investigation of any of the reports.

Not a single witness was identified by name; the commissioners said this was justified in the case of Belgians by the fear that there might be German reprisals against family members. But British soldier witnesses remained equally anonymous, for no apparent reason. Nevertheless, in his introduction, Bryce claimed that he and his fellow commissioners had tested the evidence "severely." Nobody suspected that military witnesses were not to be "tested" at all, let alone, severely so. No reason was ever given for such a grave lapse, and what Tavistock has since characterized not as a lie, but as a "misstatement."

The Bryce Report was released on May 13, 1915. British propaganda headquarters in Wellington House, near Buckingham Palace, made sure it went to virtually every newspaper in America. The impact was stupendous, as the headline and subheads in the New York Times make clear.

GERMAN ATROCITIES ARE PROVEDS
FINDS BRYCE COMMITTEE

Not Only Individual Crimes, but also
Premeditated Slaughter in Belgium

YOUNG AND OLD MUTILATED

Women Attacked, Children Brutally Slain,
Arson and Pillage Systematic

COUNTENANCED BY OFFICERS

Wanton Firing on Red Cross and White Flag:
Prisoners and Wounded Shot

CIVILIANS USED AS SHIELDS.

On May 27, 1915, Wellington House operatives in America reported to London on the outcome of their massive propaganda initiative: "Even in papers hostile to the Allies, there is not the slightest attempt to impugn the correctness of the facts alleged. Lord Bryce's prestige in America put skepticism out of the question."

Charles Masterman, chief of Wellington House, told Bryce: "Your report has swept America."

Among the small number of critics of the Bryce Report was Sir Roger Casement. "It is only necessary to turn to James Bryce, the historian, to convict Lord Bryce, the partisan," Casement wrote in a furious essay, "The Far Extended Baleful Power of the Lie."

By this time Casement had become a fierce advocate of Irish independence so few people paid any attention to his dissent, which was dismissed as biased.

Clarence Darrow, the famously iconoclastic American lawyer, who specialized in winning acquittals for ostensibly guilty clients, was another skeptic. He went to France and Belgium later in 1915 and searched in vain for a single eyewitness who could confirm even one of the Bryce stories. Increasingly dubious, Darrow announced he would pay $1,000-a very large sum in 1915 - more than $17,000 in 21st Century money - to anyone who could produce a Belgian or French boy whose hands had been amputated by a German soldier or a single child of either sex that had been bayoneted by German troops.

There were no takers, not one "victim" came forward to claim the reward although Darrow had spent a considerable amount of his own money in advertising it, far and wide.

After the war, historians who sought to examine the documentation for Bryce's stories were told that the files had mysteriously disappeared. No government official or department offered to start a search for the "missing" documents.

This blatant evasion of putting the "severely tested" documents to a newer, thoroughly impartial test prompted most historians to dismiss 99 percent of Bryce's atrocities as fabrications. One called the Report "in itself one of the worst atrocities of the war." More recent scholarship has scaled down the percentage of the Bryce report's fabrications because it turned out that several thousand Belgian civilians, including some women and children were apparently shot by the Germans in the summer of 1914 and Bryce more or less accurately summarized some of the worst excesses, such as the executions in the town of Dinant.

But even these latter day scholars admit Bryce's report was "seriously contaminated" by the rapes, amputations and speared babies. They blamed this grave lapse on hysteria, and war rage.

This amounts to giving Bryce a free pass. The number of corrections that had to be made by critics of Darrow's reports was less than one percent and failed to clear Bryce. As was pointed out at the time, 99 percent of the Bryce Commission Report were lies. Correspondence between the members of the Bryce committee survived the "disappearance" of the documents; it reveals severe doubts about the tales of mutilation and rape. These serious doubts were never spread across Britain and America in the manner of Wellington House brutality reports. One of the committee's secretaries admitted that he had been given numerous English addresses of Belgian women supposedly made pregnant by German rapes but in spite of intensive searches, was not able to locate a single one on the list.

Even the highly touted story of a Member of Parliament sheltering two pregnant women turned out to be fraudulent. Bryce apparently brushed aside this negative evidence as Bush and Blair were to do scores of times when on rare occasions, a few reporters did their job and asked awkward questions.

Lord Bryce the scholar should have known - and almost certainly did know - - that tales of spearing babies, raping and cutting off the breasts of murdered women were standard "hate - the - enemy" fables hundreds of years old, as were mass rapes in fields and public squares.

Even a cursory examination of Napoleon's campaigns in Europe brought out hundreds of these types of "atrocities," a very small fraction of which turned out to be true.

Bryce the learned historian, the learned, trusted scholar with a reputation for honesty should have rejected such fabrications out of hand. He most certainly knew that the vast majority of the "atrocity" stories emanated from Wellington House (the forerunner of the Tavistock Institute.) Instead of examining their origin and then dismissing them as propaganda, Bryce grouped them all into a "report," that found them generally factual and then issued general condemnation of the German army and people. This is reminiscent of Mr. G.W. Bush and his general classification that the entire population of several Muslim states belonged to an "Axis of Evil."

Why didn't Bryce dismiss the fabrications and concentrate on the German executions of civilians? As we have stated, he knew the bulk of the "incidents" were products of Wellington House; and had he done so, it would have opened up a very sticky subject of the wide use being made of propaganda by the British Government.

There was an important reason why Bryce chose to abandon an honorable course instead of soiling his reputation: A high percentage of the Belgian Army in 1914/1915 was made up of "Home Guards" (partisans) who wore no uniforms except for an insignia pinned to their shirts or hats. The Germans, desperately trying to win in the West before the invading Russian Army smashed through their lightly held lines in the East, were infuriated by these seemingly civilian combatants, and showed them no mercy.

That the German Army was entitled to return the fire of civilians or even initiate it by the rules of war under the Geneva Conventions applicable at that time, was never brought out in the press.

The fact is that in 1915 "partisans" right up to 1945, were fair game. Civilians, even with badges pinned to their hats were not given authority to shoot at soldiers in uniform, or afforded protection. Yes, that was what the rules of war laid out in the Geneva Conventions, and Lord Bryce and his commissioners knew it. Nor was this important fact trumpeted across England and America in the manner of the propaganda that had successfully captured the hearts and minds of the British and American people.

Some German field commanders obviously lost their heads and retaliated excessively against whole towns, such as Dinant.

But a defense of sorts could be mounted, even for these men. The ensuing debate as to what the Geneva Convention allowed would have produced yawns in newspaper readers. They wanted what Bryce gave them - blood and lust, rape and horror perpetrated by the German ("Boche") "beasts" against women and young children and "unarmed civilians." They wanted proof that the German "Hun" was a barbarian, a savage beast. And if the public had not been deceived, Wellington House, and the British Government's war effort, would have been in deep trouble.

The Bryce Report unquestionably helped England win the war. Unquestionably it swayed the opinions of the American public and convinced millions of Americans and other neutrals—it was translated into 27 languages — that the Germans were ugly beasts in human form. No one except a few "biased" outsiders such as Sir Roger Casement and Clarence Darrow ever reproached Lord Bryce for the vicious lies he had spread around the world. No fair-minded man could ever forgive Bryce for soiling himself.

Through it all, Wellington House remained in the background - few people knew of its existence - let alone its vital role, but it had done an important job and struck a mighty blow for brainwashing. As for Bryce, he went to his grave loaded with royal and academic honors, a sullied, superior liar, a man who had soiled himself and with the blood of millions on his hands, a brilliant scoundrel, a thief who stole the truth from a public entitled to know it, and who managed to evade detection and exposure and the utter condemnation that was universally afforded to Judas Iscariot.

From a perspective of a hundred years, we ought to take a much harsher view of this man. The Bryce Report had obvious connections to the British decision to maintain the blockade of Germany for seven months after the armistice in 1918, causing the starvation deaths of an estimated 600,000 elderly and very young Germans, all part of the game plan to so weaken Germany that it would never be a "threat" to the "allies" again.

The Wellington House propaganda lies about the German Army was far and away the greatest atrocity of World War I and it made every German man and woman hunger for revenge. By creating blind hatred of Germany, Bryce sowed the dragon's teeth of World War II.

CHAPTER 20

The Black Art of successful lying: Gulf War 1991

From this background, what we saw in the Gulf War circa 1991 was frightening enough to very forcefully remind us of the origin of the black art of successful lying practiced by Lord Bryce and what a congenital, witting liar he had turned out to be. It also brought to mind how Wellington House and then Tavistock set its seal on brainwashing as a tool of war. It was one of the deciding factors that made me determined to write this work and expose Tavistock and its injurious, baleful influence.

In the Gulf War the U.S. Department of Defense shut out all news media and appointed its own spokesman who gave his grossly untruthful version of events via television broadcasts. I dubbed the fellow "Pentagon Pete" and he talked blithely about "collateral damage" a new Tavistock phrase being tried for the first time ever. It took the public a long time to catch on to its meaning-human casualties, human deaths and destruction of property.

Then we had a break when CNN was allowed to come in and report on the success of the "Patriot" missile defense shooting down Iraqi SCUDS, which it turned out, was another base exercise in propaganda. According to CNN at least one SCUD attacking Israel was shot down every night. Only World In Review, in the midst of the war, reported that not a single SCUD missile had been shot down. Nobody dared to report that a total of 15 SCUDS had hit Tel Aviv and other parts of Israel. Disinformation and misinformation prevailed. Only WIR reported the truth, but with a small readership, it didn't matter to the propagandists.

Then there was the gigantic fraud perpetrated on the American people by one of the largest Public Relations companies in Washington, Hilton and Knowles.

Here again, only WIR broke the story that the whole tear- jerking episode of Iraqi soldiers pulling out new-born Kuwait babies from incubators and throwing them on the floor, was a gross falsehood. It is interesting that like Benton and Bowles, Hilton and Knowles had long ties to the Tavistock Institute. Both companies were leading "advertising" agencies.

The Hilton and Knowles fabrication, tearfully narrated by an "eye witness," (who just happened to be the teenage daughter of the Al Sabah family's Kuwaiti ambassador to Washington) was what swayed the Senate to violate the U.S. Constitution and "give" Bush the elder, "permission" to attack Iraq, despite the fact that no such provision exists in the U.S. Constitution. While Bush the elder could say; -"Well, I didn't know this, I didn't hire Hilton and Knowles," he plainly knew all about the key propaganda stunt pulled off against the American people. Nobody will ever believe that he did not recognize the sixteen-year old daughter of the Kuwaiti ambassador, who he had met before.

The Kuwaiti ambassador paid Hilton and Knowles $600,000 to stage the elaborate fraud in front of the Senate, for which he ought to have been arrested for lying to a Senate committee. What was so galling is that the daughter also went unpunished for her part in tearfully recounting her experience: "I saw the Iraqi soldiers pull the new born babies out of the incubators and thrown them on the ground," she cried.

The fact of the matter was that Narita Al Sabah had not been anywhere near Kuwait for years, and certainly not during the war! She had been in Washington D.C. with her father at the ambassador's Washington residence. Yet this child-liar and her father were not prosecuted. That is what the propaganda experts at Tavistock call "a successful remake of events." Narita Al Sabah's testimony became the centerpiece of a huge media campaign in America, and it is known to have swayed not only the Senate, but put the American people on the side of the war against Iraq.

Bush the elder indulged in an old propaganda piece in telling the world that "Saaadam" had to be removed from Iraq "to make the Middle East safe." (Remember that Wilson sent American troops to their death in France to "make the world safe for democracy.") Bush the elder suddenly began vilifying and demonizing the Iraqi president to suit the purposes of his oil cartel friends, and, as in the case of the Kaiser in 1913, it worked.

Not many people remembered the ploy put on by Wilson, otherwise they might have noticed the striking similarity in what President Bush was saying, and what Bryce told Wilson and what Wilson told the American people to sway them to support WWI. Now that Hussein is all but forgotten and the threats he allegedly posed have all been dismissed as a pack of lies, all of a sudden it is "Al Qaeda" we have to worry about.

Woodrow Wilson used plain propaganda when he told a reluctant American people that the war would "make the world safe for democracy." Bush intoned the same veritable deceit.

The cost of making the world "safe for democracy" was horrendous. Professor William Langer placed the known dead of WWI at 10,000,000 men and women soldiers and 20,000,000 wounded. Russia alone lost 9,000,000 men killed or an astonishing 75 percent of its army. The total cost of the war in dollars has been figured at $180,000,000,000 to which must be added the indirect costs of $151,612,500,000.

CHAPTER 21

The Soldiers Memorial and WWI cemeteries

The cost of the Bush war against Iraq was running at around $420 billion in mid 2005, and the Bush family wants more money for their ill-starred venture. And knowing the American people and their hapless, helpless ail-but useless representatives in the legislature, Bush will get what he wants.

The figures of the dollar cost of WWI do not tell anything about the sorrow and suffering brought to America by Wilson, the transgressor. We insert here a recent article, which gives a poignant, personal touch to the dreadful loss of life in that nightmarish war.

"Several weeks ago I visited with my family the Soldier's Memorial Museum in the heart of downtown St. Louis. It is a huge and deeply impressive building, dedicated in 1936 by President Roosevelt as a memorial to the 1075 men of St. Louis who died in the First World War. The memorial is painfully beautiful, all mosaics and marble, with terrazzo floors and Bedford stone sculptures. It is dominated by the vast black granite cenotaph in its center, covered with the hundreds of dead men's names in neat row upon row."

"On the day we visited this striking but haunted place it seemed completely empty. While empty of visitors, it was, however, full of the spirits and voices and faces of the pale, tousled-headed boys in neatly-pressed uniforms, who had marched off from St. Louis 86 years ago to fight in a glorious war so far away in a far-off land, boys who had never come back home.

The poignancy of that was rendered all the stronger by the fact that we are living daily with the repercussions of current conflict, the savage bloody war in Iraq. We read daily of the boys who will never come back home."

"What struck me most as I walked around the memorial and the museum, holding my newborn baby girl, was the fact that it looked like so many memorials that I had visited in my home country of Scotland. It also looked like those I had visited in France, in England and in Canada and New Zealand and it looked just like the memorials in almost every other country touched by the carnage of World War One."

"In almost every country touched by the carnage of WWI, the so-called "War to End all Wars;" men rushed to join the military and marched off to war with great enthusiasm. They believed it would be a short, sharp and successful war, fought for good reasons, and glorious for the winners. They believed they were building a better world."

"They were wrong. An average of 5,500 men died every single day for four and a half years in the First World War; that is roughly four men per minute, every minute, for four and a half years, until 10 million men were dead. The First World War did more than destroy lives; it destroyed the confidence in progress, in prosperity and in reasonableness of civilized human beings that had become so characteristic of the nineteenth century. The war destroyed much of the next generation which would have provided leadership to Europe..."

"And this morning, as I sit holding my baby girl I read daily reports of escalating violence in Iraq, with British, Iraqi and American men continuing to die, the St. Louis Soldier's - a memorial to a war that should have never been fought - haunts me and their ghosts haunt the Memorial. It was the worst of all disasters, the war that should have never been fought-haunts me."

"The Neo-Conservative brains in the U.S. Administration would have been wise to visit places like this and think long and hard about the lessons of such memorials before embarking on a war in the Middle East that has already killed an unknown number of people and which will certainly kill many more, directly and indirectly.

(Written by Professor Dr. James Lachlan MacLeod, Associate Professor of History, University of Evansville, Indiana).

My experiences parallel those of Professor MacLeod. I visited the battlefields of Verdun and Passchendale where most of the slaughter he so ably recounts, occurred. I tried to imagine 10 million soldiers dying so young, the terror, the horror and the sorrow they experienced, and the inconsolable sorrow of the ones they left behind. While standing in the afternoon's fading light in one of the many war cemeteries in France, and looking upon the thousands upon thousands of neat white crosses marching across the war cemeteries, I was overcome by anger and then overwhelmed by grief, so much so that I swear I heard the cries and the shouts of anguish of the dead calling for justice to be done, so cruelly cut down in their prime, and seemed to see their faces reflected in the clouds above.

It was a mystical experience I will never forget, much like the experience of a British officer who visited these battlefields in 1919:

Yesterday I visited the battlefields of the last years. The place was scarcely recognizable. Instead of a wilderness of ground torn up by shells, the round was a garden of wild flowers and tall grasses. Most remarkable of all was the appearance of many thousands of white butterflies which fluttered around. It was as if the souls of the dead soldiers had come to haunt the spot where so many fell. It was eerie to see them. And the silence! It was so still that I could almost hear the beat of the butterflies' wings. (From records in the British War Museum in London)

My intense feelings of outrage made me determined to find out everything I could about a terrible war that began with massive gout of propaganda, the scourge of the modern world. It was another decisive reason for writing this book and exposing the evil of Tavistock. Sir Roger Casement thought Lord Bryce ought to have been hanged for treason and I feel Wilson ought to have suffered a similar fate, which would have stopped Roosevelt and Churchill from plunging the world into a second round of carnage. Propaganda prevailed, and the western civilized world was lost.

The world we knew, the world established by western civilization, is gone. Spengler's gloomy predictions proved right. In place of our western civilized world we shall soon see the ghastly edifice of the new Communist Socialist One World Government looming up through the darkness of the coming long night.

Let there be no doubt that the First World War was caused by Britain and her ally, the United States of America with the aide of Wellington House. The war could not have been mounted without the dark forces of Wellington House. The name of Lord Grey, its principal architect will go down in history as traitorous dishonest politician.

There is no consensus as to why Britain started WWI. But by 1916, the German Army had defeated the French and British armies in a most decisive manner. Wilson was under heavy pressure to get American troops shipped to Europe, so Wellington House unleashed an all-out propaganda war against the American people, but which nevertheless, remained ineffective until the Bryce Report was published.

To understand what is happening in Iraq is impossible unless we make ourselves fully cognizant with the terrible propaganda deployed against the British and American people in 1913 and 1940. It was one of the darkest and most foul chapters in history, with Wilson mouthing such lies as a" just war", and "a war to end all wars", a war "to make the world safe for democracy." What the war was about was to make trade safe for Britain especially, and France now being threatened by German industry.

But they were words in obfuscation of his true intent and meaningless in that context, just what you'd expect from a politician. The kind of bunkum one find's on a society page.

Wilson's talk of "making the world safe for democracy" was nothing more than colored gas bubbles. He was proposing to go into the war on the side of the English, who were at that very moment making sure there was no popular democracy in the Empire.

The English had just brutally finished off the Boers in South Africa in a cruel war that lasted three years. If Wilson wanted to make the world "safe for democracy", he ought to have gone to war on the side of Germany against England, the aggressor and instigator of the war.

Instead of "making the world safe for democracy" it turned out to be the greatest calamity ever to befall civilized nations that had fallen into the clutches of men who were corrupt immoral liars, into a war quite properly called, "The Great War." It was of course only "great" in its size and scope.

We will never understand how the United States became the "sole great power," unless we confess to the sins of Wilson and the British establishment of 100 years ago. The United States has continuously entangled itself in the affairs of other sovereign nation's affairs, despite the dire warning of George Washington, and the first instance of this was our entry into WWI and the failed League of Nations. Wilson made full use of the master propagandists of Wellington House using sloganeering as a sword, told the reluctant Senate that if it did not ratify the League of Nations "it will break the heart of the world."

Thanks to Senator Cabot Lodge, and a number of U.S. Senators who after sober reflection and examination of the U.S. Constitution, declined to ratify the League of Nations treaty because they discovered it sought to kill U.S. sovereignty. Using and abusing his penchant for propaganda, Wilson tried to carry the day by declaring his re-election campaign "a great and solemn referendum for acceptance of the treaty" but not having Lord Bryce to back him, lost, and was swept away.

Unfortunately it did not take the pliers of propaganda long to stage a comeback with the revamped United Nations version of the League of Nations. Truman, (not the simple hat seller from Missouri but the Master Mason) betrayed the American people by permitting this one-world edifice in the U.S. and Truman used propaganda left over by Wilson to persuade key senators to vote for his lies.

What Truman did was force the American nation to enter into a pact with the devil-the devil of power over justice and truth, justice from the barrel of a gun. We applied that "justice" in WWII through mass bombing of civilian centers without regard to loss of life and we used atomic bombs on Japan, although the war was over, in the propaganda ploy of "shock and awe" echoed by Rumsfeld in the unconstitutional war against Iraq.

CHAPTER 22

Peace is not popular

The Second World War followed an almost identical pattern as WWI. For concluding a peace deal with Hitler, Neville Chamberlain was at once subjected to a mighty propaganda barrage directed by the Tavistock Institute. Chamberlain had defied the Committee of 300 and backed a newcomer, a rank outsider who was seen as a threat to world Socialism.

The world did not learn the truth about Chamberlain or that he was an able politician bent upon avoiding another war, or that he was well experienced and had worked out an equitable peace plan - which of course - did not suit the munitions merchants vultures sitting on the fence waiting to pick clean the wealth of nations and the corpses of their sons.

The vast propaganda machine set up at the Tavistock Institute in London immediately swung into action against Chamberlain, after he announced his successful peace plan. Shakespeare said that "the evil that men do lives after them; the good is oft interred with their bones." The good done by Chamberlain did not suit the warmongers and they buried Chamberlain under a catalogue of propaganda and outright lies.

These lies were the work of specialists in propaganda employed at the Tavistock Institute, notably, Peter Howard, Michael Foot and Frank Owen. One of these men, employing the pen-name of "Cato" so vilified Chamberlain that the odium they attached to his name lives even to this day in July of 2005. Such is the power of the might Tavistock propaganda machine.

In later years, long after the deceitful propaganda experts had done their work, British historian and scholar David Dutton wrote a book, Neville Chamberlain in which he gave a balanced assessment of the former prime minister.

Far from being a "dupe of Hitler" and "a fool" Chamberlain showed considerable negotiating skill and was a highly competent leader, who fought valiantly to prevent another war. But that ran contrary to the wishes of the Committee of 300. Churchill got his "delicious war," but by 1941, the "Allies" had virtually been driven off the continent of Europe with huge loss of manpower. France, Belgium, Holland and Denmark were occupied.

Germany offered generous terms to England but warmonger Churchill rejected peace overtures, and turned to his old workhorse ally, the United States, to provide men, money and materials to continue "the delicious war."

To the American people we say in deep sorrow: "When will you ever learn? When are you going to distinguish between propaganda and genuine information? When are you going to put proposal for war to the constitutional test?"

Wilson was a consummate liar and a hater of the U.S. Constitution; yet, thanks to a huge propaganda drive organized run and maintained by Wellington House, he was able to accomplish his mission by operating under a banner of patriotism, which overcame vigorous opposition to the war. Between Wilson, Churchill and Roosevelt, tremendous damage was done to western Christian civilization. Yet in spite of this fact, a wave of propaganda continues to wash over their names, as if to rid them of the blood on of millions on their hands.

Instead of being vilified, numerous monuments to their honor are to be found all over Europe, and in America a multi- billion dollar monument is to be erected in honor of Franklin D. Roosevelt, whose treason engineered the Japanese "to fire the first shot" as the Stimson Dairies record. Pearl Harbor opened the way to Communist control of China, and ultimately the way to a new Communist-Socialist New World Order inside a One World Government. Our only hope in a vale of despair is that this work might help to open the eyes of the American people, so that they will resolve never again to fall for propaganda, although in the wake of the 9/11 tragedy, it now seems a vain hope.

We recently lived through the disturbing experience of being rushed into an unnecessary war in Serbia, Afghanistan and Iraq through the expanded propaganda tools in the hands of Tavistock's experts, the same tool used to vilify the Kaiser and Chamberlain. President Milosevic was demonized vilified, belittled and finally driven from office. President Milosevic was illegally arrested and illegally transported to Holland for "trail" by a kangaroo court that has been trying for nearly four years to convict him of "war crimes."

George Bush the younger refused to give the mediators in Iraq time to work because he knew that it would prevent war. He refused to give the UN weapons inspectors to complete their work, and instead, declared with the evil intent of all propagandists that the world could not wait for ten day more because of the "imminent danger" posed by the "Weapons of Mass Destruction" in the hands of "the Iraqi dictator." (The "Butcher of Baghdad.")

Thus, once again, the people of the United States were swept along by a flood tide of naked lies put out by the propagandists at Tavistock Institute and echoed by the American media, especially the chief propaganda organ in the United States, Fox News Channel.

In one respect Americans are more fortunate this time: We have not had to wait for a 100 years to pass for the truth to come out: There were no "Weapons of Mass Destruction", no "chemical and bacteriological factories," no long range rockets to cause a "mushroom cloud over Boston," (courtesy of the apologist for Tavistock propaganda and mass brainwashing, Ms. Rice), and Mr. Bush and his copartner in crime, British Prime Minister Blair. But in spite of being caught in a web of lies, all the abovementioned remain in office. They have not been sacked for the scores of lies they swore was the truth, and from which they are now not even bothering to extricate themselves, shrugging of criticism with the help of spin masters (polished liars) like Karl Rove and Alaister Campbell. Let us hope that the cause of justice will be served, and that those responsible for the tragedy of the bombing of Serbia and Afghanistan, and the unwarranted invasions of Iraq will be brought before the bar of international justice to account for their crimes.

The voices of the dead cry out from the battlefields of Europe, the Pacific, from Serbia and Afghanistan; and from Iraq, lamenting that they died because "brainwashing" triumphed and propaganda prevailed, the scourge of the modern world, rolling out from the Tavistock Institute like some foul miasma from a dank and noisome bog, enveloping the world, blinding it to the truth.

WELLINGTON HOUSE PROPAGANDA STARS

Lord Northcliffe.

Walter Lippman.

Edward Bernays and
Eleanor Roosevelt.

Edward Bernays.

Social Science scientists at Tavistock

W.R. Bion.

Gregory Bateson.

R.D. Laing.

Eric L. Trist. Social Science
scientist at Tavistock
Institute.

Leon Trotsky. Marxist
leader (Real name Lev.
Bronstein.)

Willy Munzenberg. The
brilliant Russian spy and
leading propagandist.

Lord Northcliffe and Adolph Hitler.

George Bernard Shaw. Irish
Playwright and Fabianist.

H.G. Wells. British Author.
Leading Fabianist, and secret
service agent. Wrote War of
Worlds.

Walter Rathenau. Leading
German industrialist. Financial
advisor to Kaiser Wilhelm II.

Lord Bertrand
Russell. British
Socialist, Author, and
Elder Statesman of
the "300."

Kaiser Wilhelm II
Wellington House falsely
maligned the German
leader as a "Bloody
Butcher."

Queen Victoria, was a
cousin of Wilhelm II.

King George V.

Woodrow Wilson U.S.
President. An avowed
Socialist.

The infamous propaganda drawing depicting Kaiser Wilhelm II standing over Belgian women and children he had shot. This drawing and one like it produced by Wellington House with Wilhelm II standing over Belgian children with a sword dripping in blood from their severed hands, appeared in newspapers across Britain and the United States.

(above) Trotsky "reviews" his "troops" in Moscow. This is one of the hundreds of propaganda photographs that flooded willing Western newspapers.

(below) A depiction of one of the scores of dreadful hand to-hand battles of WWI. The brutality and slaughter left survivors on both sides mentally crippled and haunted by what they had experienced.

(1) Sean Hannity. (2) Rush Limbaugh.

(3) Tucker Carlson. (4) Matt Drudge.

(5) G. Gordon Liddy. (6) Peggy Noonan.

(7) Brian Williams. (8) Bill O'Reilly.

(9) Lawrence Kudlow. (10) Dick Morris.

(11) John Stossel. (12) William Bennet.

(13) Oliver North. (14) Michael Savage.

(15) Michael Reagan. (16) Joe Scarborough.

CHAPTER 23

The Tavistock Institute: Britain's control of the United States

The Tavistock Institute of Human Relations is situated in London and on the grounds of Sussex University, Sussex, England, where most of its research facilities are located. Tavistock remains as important today as it was when I first revealed its existence early in 1969. I have been accused of having been a part of Tavistock because I worked in close proximity to Tavistock's Sussex facility, and knew so much of its history.

Most of Tavistock's more recent activity has had, and is still having, a profound influence upon the way we live in America, and upon our political institutions. Tavistock is believed to be behind the pro-abortion publicity, the proliferation of drugs, sodomy and lesbianism, family traditions, and the fierce attack on the Constitution, our misconduct in foreign policy and our economic system, programmed to fail.

Apart from John Rawlings Reese no two men made such a difference to world politics and world events as shaped at Tavistock than Edward Bernays (the double nephew of Sigmund Freud) and Kurt Lewin. A "third man" must be included here, although he was never on the faculty at Tavistock and I refer to Willi Munzenberg whose propaganda methods and applications so crucial to the modern age of mass communication earned him the title, "the greatest propagandist in the world." Undoubtedly the most brilliant man of his era, (he began his work before WWI) Munzenberg was responsible for sanitizing the Bolsheviks after they overthrew the Romanov Dynasty.

Munzenberg definitely shaped the ideas and methods put into practice by Bernays and Lewin. His legendary exploits in handling Leon Tepper the Kappelmeister of the Rot Kappell (Conductor of the "Red Orchestra" spy ring) made Munzenberg the master spy of every intelligence agency in existence. Tepper was trained by Munzenberg and he never got caught. Tepper was able to obtain all of the secrets of Britain and the United States in WWII. There was hardly a single secret plan the "allies" launched that was not already known to Tepper, who passed the information to the KGB and the GRU in Moscow.

In his field, Bernays was equally brilliant but I suspect that most of his ideas originated with his famous uncle Sigmund. As for his ideas on propaganda, there is little doubt that he "borrowed" from Munzenberg and this is reflected in the Bernays classic Propaganda that was published in 1928. The thesis of the book is that it is entirely proper and a natural right for government to organize public opinion to conform to official policies. We shall return to this subject later.

Munzenberg was bold enough to put his basic tenets about propaganda into practice well before Bernays, or Joseph Goebbels, the German Minister of Popular Enlightenment (as the Ministry of Propaganda was called.)

The propaganda specialist of the Nazi Party greatly admired Munzenberg's work and modeled his own propaganda program closely upon Munzenberg's methods. Goebbels always took care to credit Munzenberg as the "father" of propaganda even when few knew very little about him.

Goebbels had made a particular study of how Munzenberg had used his mastery of the science of propaganda when Lenin drafted him to blunt the appalling publicity generated in 1921, when 25 millions peasants in the Volga region died from the ravages of famine. Thus it came about that German born Munzenberg became the darling of the Bolshevik. To quote from a recent history account:

"Munzenberg, who by then had returned to Berlin where he was later elected to the Reichstag as a Communist deputy, was charged with setting up a bogus 'charity', the Foreign Committee for the Organization of Worker Relief for the Hungry in the Soviet Union, the purpose of which was to pretend to the world that humanitarian relief was coming from a source other than Herbert Hoover's American Relief Organization. In this Munzenberg was altogether successful."

Munzenberg gained the attention of the directorate of the former Wellington House which in 1921 had changed its name to the Tavistock Institute of Human Relations under the direction of Major General John Rawlings Reese, formerly of the British Army Psychological Warfare Bureau School.

It will not come as a surprise to readers who have followed my work that much of the techniques adopted and perfected by Munzenberg were adopted by Bernays and his colleagues, Kurt Lewin, Eric Trist, Dorwin Cartwright, and H.V. Dicks W.R. Bion at Tavistock, who then taught the methods to the Central Intelligence Agency.

Munzenberg was not the only Communist to profoundly influence events in the United States. I happen to believe that Tavistock aided in preparing the "abortion brief," that was subsequently presented to the Supreme Court in 1973,

as an original work, when in fact, it was merely a recital of what Madame Kollontei, the founder of the "women's liberation " movement and "free love" proponent in the USSR had written.

A Bolshevik commissar and leading light, her book is a diatribe against the sanctity of marriage and the family as the most important social unit in Christian countries. Kollontei, of course, took her "feminism" straight from the pages of the Communist

Manifesto of 1848.

George Orwell, the MI6 operative who wrote the famous 1984 had studied the work of Munzenberg in great detail. In fact his best-known statement was based on what Munzenberg had said was the basis of propaganda:

"Political language is designed to make lies sound truthful and murder respectable and to give the appearance of solidity to pure wind."

As his German counterpart Munzenberg said: "All news is lies and all propaganda is disguised as news."

It is useful to know about Munzenberg as it helps us to understand how politicians operate and how secret forces control access to information, and how public opinion is shaped and molded. Bernays certainly followed the master and never deviated from his methodology. Without knowing these things, we can never understand how President George Bush is able to do the things he does and not have to face the consequences. It has certainly enabled me to trace the origin of the so-called "Neo-Conservatives" that shape his policies, right back to its founder, Irving Kristol who admits to having been an avowed follower of Leon Trotsky.

Tavistock remains the mother of all research facilities connected with behavior modifications, opinion making and shaping of political events. What Tavistock did was to create a "black hole of deception in the 20th century." Its task would have been made a great deal more difficult had it not been for the prostitution of the media and its role in disseminating "the gospel according to George Orwell."

Lord Northcliffe the chief of Tavistock's predecessor, Wellington House, had been a media mogul and at one stage went so far as to ship thousands of copies of his Daily Mail to France each week and then have them delivered by a fleet of motor trucks to British troops at the front lines, "to win their hearts and minds in support of the war" (WWI).

Especially here in the United States, it has virtually taken over the Massachusetts Institute of Technology (MIT), Stanford Research, Esalen Institute, the Wharton School of Economics, Hudson Institute, Kissinger Associates, Duke University, and many more institutions we have come to think of as wholly American.

The Rand Research and Development Corporation, under the tutelage of Tavistock has had a profound influence on so many institutions and segments of our society. As one of the principal research institutions directly controlled by Tavistock, Rand runs our ICBM program, does prime analyses for U.S. foreign policy makers, and advises on nuclear policies, does hundreds of projects for the C.I. A. in the field of mind control.

Some of Rand's clients include AT&T, Chase Manhattan Bank, the U.S. Air Force, the U.S. Department of Energy and B.M. Rand is one of the major Tavistock-controlled institutions in the world, and working on brainwashing at all levels, including government, military, religious organizations. The Anglican Church's Desmond Tutu was one of Rand's projects.

Take another example; Georgetown University, perhaps one of the top institutions of higher learning in America. Starting in 1938, the entire structure of Georgetown was made over by Tavistock - all of its learning formats and programs altered to suit a blueprint drawn up by Tavistock's "brain trust team."

This has had great significance for U.S. policies, especially in the area of foreign policy relations. Without exception, United States State Department field officers are trained at Georgetown.

Some of Georgetown's (Tavistock) better-known graduates are

Richard Armitage and Henry Kissinger. Just how much damage these two members of the John Rawlings Reese Invisible Army have done to the well-being of our country will have to be told at another time.

There is mounting evidence of increased input into our intelligence agencies by Tavistock. When we think of intelligence in the U.S. we generally think of the CJA or Division Five of the FBI.

But there are a great many other intelligence agencies receiving instruction from Tavistock. These include the Defense Department Intelligence (DIA), the National Reconnaissance Office (NRO), and the Office of Naval Intelligence (ONI,) the Treasury Intelligence Service (TIS), the State Department Intelligence Service, the Drug Enforcement Agency (DEA) and at least ten others.

How and when did Tavistock begin its career? As I said in my 1969 and 1983 works, when we think of Tavistock we automatically think of its founder, British Army Major John Rawlings Reese. Up until 1969, there were very few people in Britain outside of intelligence circles, who knew of the existence of Tavistock, let alone what was being done at its facilities in London and Sussex.

Tavistock provided services of a sinister nature to those people we find in every city across this land; people who have local and state government officials and police departments in the palm of their hand.

This is the case in every major American city also, where the Illuminati members of Freemasonry use their secret powers of control, to walk all over the Bill of Rights, intimidating and brutalizing innocent citizens at will. Where are the statesmen who once made this country great? What we have in their place are lawmakers who do not enforce the laws they make, and who are terrified to correct the obvious wrongs that abound on every hand, afraid, because if they obeyed their oath of office, they might find themselves without a job.

They are also lawmakers who do not have even the vaguest idea of what Constitutional law is, and they do not seem to care. They pass "laws" that were never tested as to their constitutionality. The majority of the legislators do not know how to do this, anyway. As a result, anarchy prevails in Washington. It may well come as a shock to most candidates who run for the House and Senate, that each and every one of them is carefully checked and profiled by the behavior modification scientists at Tavistock, or one or more of its affiliates in the U.S. Any candidate who is pliable to suggestions and found to be easy to control is "puffed."

Suffice to say that a spirit of unconstitutional lawlessness pertains in the Congress, which is why we are insulted by such measures as the "Brady" bill and the Feinstein "assault weapons" bill.

"Assault weapons" and in 2003 the "Homeland Security Bill" and the "Patriot Act," do not appear anywhere in the Constitution and all are, therefore, a prohibition. Feinstein's "law" looks suspiciously like the work of the Tavistock Institute. The Constitution being the supreme law of the land, "gun control" laws are null and void.

Guns are private property. Guns do not come under Interstate Commerce. Every U.S. citizen of sound mind, of legal age and not a felon has the right to keep and bear arms in any quantity and in any place.

This was stated by the great St. George Tucker who declared:

"The Congress of the United States possesses no power to regulate or interfere with the domestic concerns of any of the States, it belongs to them (the States) to establish any rules respecting the right of property, nor will the Constitution permit any prohibition of arms to the people or peaceful assembly by them for whatever purpose and in any number, whatsoever they may see the occasion." (Blackstone's Views on the Constitution, page 315)

Any candidate who is not going to be easy to control or who does not fit the Tavistock profiles is ushered out. In this, the print and electronic media— under Tavistock's direction—or one of its affiliates, plays a key role. Let the voter beware, let the public beware.

Our election process has become a farce, thanks to the work done by Tavistock in controlling the thoughts and ideas of the people of this nation by means of "inner directional conditioning" and "long distance penetration" of which the mind-control science of polling is an integral part. Tavistock serves the Black Nobility in all of its elements, working to rob us of the victory of the American Revolution of 1776. If the reader is unfamiliar with the Black Nobility, of course, the term does not refer to black people. It refers to a group of extremely wealthy people, dynasties, whose history dates back for more than five hundred years and who make up the backbone of the Committee of 300.

On the international front, as well as in areas of those institutions in the U.S. who decide foreign policy, Tavistock does psychological profiling at all levels of government, as well as intruding into private life, on a truly vast scale.

Tavistock developed profiles and programs for the Club of Rome, the Cini Foundation, the German Marshall fund, the Rockefeller Foundation, the Bilderbergers, the CFR and the Trilateral Commission, the Ditchley Foundation, the Bank of International Settlements, the I.M.F. the United Nations and the World Bank, Microsoft, Citibank, the New York Stock Exchange and so on. This is by no means a complete list of institutions in the hands of Tavistock planners.

The propaganda barrage that preceded the 1991 Bush Gulf War was based around a psychological profile of huge population groups in the U.S. prepared by Tavistock. The results were passed on to the opinion makers, also known as "advertising agencies" on Madison Avenue.

So effective was this propaganda, that within two weeks, people who didn't even know where Iraq was on the map, let alone who its leaders were, began to shout and clamor for war against "a dictator who threatens America's interests." Frightening? YES, but unfortunately 100 percent true! The very words "gulf crisis" were crafted by Tavistock Institute to arouse maximum support for the Bush war on behalf of a Committee of 300-flagship company, British Petroleum (BP).

We now know—at least some of us know—just what a big role Tavistock plays when it comes to creating public opinion based on obfuscation, lies, dissembling, misrepresentation and outright fraud. There isn't any other institution in the world that can hold a candle to the Tavistock Institute for Human Relations. Quoting from my updated 1984 report:

"There are a few institutions and publishing businesses that are catching on to the changes that are occurring. The latest issue of "Esquire Magazine" carries an article entitled "Discovering America." 'Esquire' did not mention Tavistock by name, but this is what it said: During the social revolution (a very significant phrase) of the 70s, most of the rituals and personal inter-action and the institutional life were radically altered. Naturally, these changes have affected the way we perceive the future... The economic base of America is changing and new services and products are being offered."

The article then went on to state that our professional lives, our leisure time, our educational systems are being altered, and more importantly, the thinking of our children is being altered. The writer of the "Esquire" article concluded:

"America is being transformed as is the direction it will take in the future...Occasionally our new American section (promised for future editions of Esquire), won't seem so new, since most of the new thinking has been creeping into the main stream of American life, but until now, it has gone unnoticed."

I could not have given a more fitting description of the fallacy "time changes things." Nothing changes on its own, all changes are engineered, whether in secret or in public. While "Esquire" didn't say who is responsible for the changes - for the most part about unwanted changes - that We, the People, attempted to resist. (Capitals intended.)

"Esquire" is not alone in its contention. Millions of American is living in total ignorance of the forces shaping their future. They are unaware that America is being thoroughly "conditioned" by Tavistock's "inner directional long range penetration method." The worst part of it is that these millions, because of Tavistock conditioning (making Americans think in the way Tavistock would have them think), no longer seem to care. They have been "Inner Conditioned" through "Long Range Penetration"—the master control plan set up by Tavistock to brainwash the nation for so long that they now suffer a constant state of "shellshock."

As we shall see, there is good reason for this apathy and ignorance. The unwanted, forced changes we have been subjected to as a nation, were the work of several master theoreticians and technicians who joined John Rawlings Reese at the Tavistock Institute.

CHAPTER 24

Brainwashing saves a U.S. President

I would venture to suggest that even after all my years of exposing Reese and his work; fully 95 percent of Americans don't know who he is or what harm he has done to the United States.

This substantial number of our citizens is even today totally unaware of how they have been manipulated and forced to accept "new ideas", "new cultures", and "new religions". They have been grossly violated and don't know it. They are still being violated and still don't know what is happening, especially when it comes to opinion making through polling.

To illustrate my contention, former President Clinton was able to survive scandal after scandal on the basis of the polls showing that the American people didn't care enough about his outlandish behavior to call for impeachment proceedings. Could this be right? Could it be true that people really don't care about public morals anymore? Of course not!

The situation is a contrived one taught by Tavistock Institute and every polltaker is trained in Tavistock methods of opinion making and manipulation of public opinion, so that the answers "come out right."

We can add President G.W. Bush to the "survivors". He has not been removed from office notwithstanding the blatant lies that were used to start an illegal (unconstitutional) in Iraq. It is unconstitutional because war was never constitutionally declared.

Also, there is no provision in the U.S. Constitution for the United States to attack another nation that has not committed acts of belligerency against it. How has President Bush got away with not being impeached? The answers lie in the Tavistock Institute and its mass brainwashing capabilities.

One of the early tasks undertaken by Tavistock after it launched total war on the U.S. in 1946 was to force acceptance of "alternate life styles" on the American people. Tavistock documents showed how the leaders of a campaign to force legal public acceptance of groups, whose behavior was until the changes were forced through by the Congress, recognized as a crime in almost every State in the Union, and in some States, remains as a crime. I am referring to the "gay lifestyle" as it has come to be known.

The careful profiling that was done before this "change" program was launched was not believed by the uninitiated, who dismissed it as "lurid science fiction", even though it were spelled out in the simplest of terms. A vast majority of Americans never heard (and still do not know in 2005) that the Tavistock Institute went to war against them in 1946, nor that the people have been losing that war ever since.

Tavistock turned its attention to the United States at the close of WWII. The methods that brought Germany down, were now unleashed against the United States. The massive brainwashing of our nation was called "Long Range Penetration " and "Inner Directional Conditioning."

The main purpose of this endeavor was to install Socialist programs at every level of government; ushering in the New Dark Age a New World Order inside a One World Government Communist dictatorship.

Particularly, it was designed to break down the sanctity of

marriage and family life. And it was aimed at the Constitution, also, to "make it of no effect." Homosexuality, lesbianism, and abortion are Tavistock-designed programs, as are aimed at "changing" the U.S. Constitution.

Much of Tavistock's programs are based on getting the "right" candidates elected; this being achieved with the help of its trained pollsters with their cleverly loaded questions. Tavistock's "gay lifestyle" blueprint called for several "task force" units who would assist the media in painting over the homosexual onslaught and making the "new lifestyle" crusaders seem "just like any other people."

"Talk shows" are now an integral part of such plans, but back then, they were not as widely used to bring about social changes as they are today. The leaders selected by Tavistock to promote tremendous changes on the social and political scene via talk shows, were Phil Donahue and Geraldo Riviera, Bill O'Reilly, Barbara Walters and scores of other people whose names have become household names in America. It was they who presented people who were to run for office; people who hitherto, would have been laughed off the platform. But now, thanks to the skillful use of polling, such persons are taken seriously.

The minuscule planning that went into priming the public through T.V. talk show hosts, cost millions of dollars spent in putting this Tavistock-forced social change long-range plan into effect, and as the results show, Tavistock did its homework well. With all of my experience, I am still amazed at how this great coup was pulled off.

Entire communities across the nation were profiled; guests for talk shows and their audiences were selected by profile matching, without ever being aware of what was being done without their knowledge and consent. Americans were bamboozled on a grand scale and didn't know it then and still don't know it! Nor did they know that they were being whipsawed by the Tavistock Institute for Human Relations.

Finally, after three years of preparation, the Tavistock sodomist/lesbian onslaught that was launched against a totally unsuspecting American people can be likened to the storm that burst upon the unsuspecting French nation at the time of the French Revolution.

The well-planned and executed campaign began in Florida, according to plan, and, exactly as planned, Anita Bryant came forward to take up the cudgels against the invaders from the "gay community" - words carefully selected by Tavistock, which have now become fully acceptable. Before this episode, the word "gay" was never used to describe homosexuals or their behavior.

Tavistock was founded in 1921 as a successor to Wellington House that had pulled off a great coup in 1914 and 1917, and as already related, getting Britain and America into a savage war against Germany.

Tavistock was to serve as a primary research vehicle for British intelligence services, still the best in the world. Major, later Brigadier General John Rawlings Reese commissioned by the monarch was chosen to run the project and the British royal family funded the project with help from the Rockefellers and the Rothschilds.

In the middle of WWII, Tavistock received additional funding from David Rockefeller, in return for help in taking over the former Reynard Heydrich's German secret intelligence service. The whole apparatus and personnel of the brilliant top Nazi security service was bodily transported to Washington, D.C., in violation of the supreme law of the land. It now began to be called "Interpol."

During the Second World War, both the London and Sussex facilities of Tavistock, served as headquarters for the British

Army's Psychological Warfare Bureau.

The significance of this is that through the "best friend" arrangement between Churchill and Roosevelt, Tavistock was able to take full control of U.S. intelligence and military policies through Special Operations Executive (SOE) and maintained this control throughout the Second World War. Eisenhower was selected by the Committee of 300 to become the commanding general of the allied forces in Europe, but only after extensive profiling by Tavistock. He was then appointed to the White House. Eisenhower was allowed to retain his seat in the White House until, with his usefulness expended, as memories of the war receded, he was dumped. Eisenhower's bitterness over the treatment he received at the hands of the Committee of 300 and the Tavistock Institute is reflected in his statements about the dangers posed by the military-industrial complex--a veiled reference to his former bosses, the "Olympians."

The "Committee of 300" book, tells the full story of this hitherto ultra-secret, ultra-elite body of men who rule the world. The Committee of 300 has at its disposal a vast, interlocking network of banks, finance houses, the print and electronic media, large groups of "think tanks", new science scientists who are in reality the modern-day creators of what passes for public opinion created through its national poll opinion makers, and so on. Today, over 450 of the top Fortune 500 companies are in the grip of the Committee of 300.

These include Petro-Canada, the Hong Kong and Shanghai Bank, Halliburton, Root, Kellogg and Brown, British Petroleum, Shell, Xerox, Rank, Raytheon, ITT, Eagle Insurance, all the largest insurance companies, all of the top companies and or organizations in the U.S., Britain and Canada. The so-called environmental movement is entirely controlled by the Committee, through the Tavistock Institute.

Most people tend to believe that "brainwashing" is a

Korean/Chinese technique. It isn't. Brainwashing dates back to Tavistock as the originator of the art. The science of behavioral modifications had its origin in Tavistock, which trained an army of intelligence personnel to go out and do likewise.

The United States, perhaps more than any other country, has felt the weight of Tavistock's fist in our national life at almost every level, and its grip on this country has not been lessened: If anything, with the advent of William Jefferson Clinton, and Bush, father and son, it has been considerably tightened. We were truly brainwashed in 1992 and 1996. We are truly a brainwashed nation in 2005. The United States is the principal victim of long-range penetration warfare using the Reese techniques.

Other victim-countries are Rhodesia (now Zimbabwe,) Angola, South Africa, the Philippines, South Korea, Central America, Iran, Iraq, Serbia, Yugoslavia, and Venezuela.

The technique isn't working in Iraq and Iran, and by and large, Muslim countries seem less receptive to Tavistock mass population control methods than Western countries.

There is no doubt that their strict adherence to the laws of the Koran and their Islamic faith is what foiled Tavistock's plans for the Middle East, at least, temporarily. Therefore, a concerted drive was mounted to wage war on the Muslim world.

That Reese succeeded in forcing changes on a large number of countries is mirrored in events that have since transpired. At home, Tavistock reshaped a whole series of major U.S. institutions, both private and government, among them our intelligence agencies, units of the Pentagon, Congressional committees, large corporations, the entertainment world, and so on.

CHAPTER 25

Tavistock's assault on the U.S.

One of the major players in the Tavistock team was Dr. Kurt Lewin. Born in Germany, but forced to flee when his population control experiments were discovered by the German government. Lewin was already well known to Reese—the two having cooperated extensively in experiments in polling and similar opinion-shaping experiments. It is said that Dr. Goebbels enthusiastically embraced Tavistock methods.

Lewin fled to England, where he joined Reese at Tavistock and was given his first major task: Propagandize America into the Second World War, by launching a media blitz against Germany in both Europe and the U.S. He succeeded admirably in what turned out to be the largest propaganda campaign in history, one that whipped the American people into a frenzy of hatred against Germany, and later, Japan. The blitz eventually cost the lives of hundreds of thousands of American soldiers and poured billions of dollars into the coffers of the Wall Street and international banks and the arms merchants.

Our loss in lives and national treasures cannot be recovered.

Just prior to the assault on Iraq, the U.S. was subjected to a propaganda blast only slightly below the level of that which was developed to shove the United States into the Second World War. Careful analyses of key words and phrases developed by Lewin for WWII use, showed that in 93.6 percent of all cases examined, these trigger-words and phrases matched up with those used in the Korean War, the Vietnam War and the Gulf War.

In the Vietnam War era, polling using Tavistock methodology was used with devastating effect against the American people.

During the Gulf War, an example of Tavistock methods was the way the State Department kept on referring to its embassy staff in Kuwait as "hostages", although none were ever imprisoned. In fact, every single one of them was free to leave at any time, but were ordered to remain in Kuwait so that propaganda could be made out of their situation.

In essence, the "hostages" were hostages of the State Department! Unable to goad President Hussein into firing the first shots, another "contrived situation" like Pearl Harbor had to be mounted. April Glaspie's name will forever be associated with treachery and infamy. What followed was an elaborate theft of millions of barrels of Iraqi oil by Kuwait. Hussein was given the "all clear" by U.S. ambassador to Baghdad April Gillespie, to attack Iraq and put an end to a situation that was costing the Iraqi people billions of dollars. But when the attack was mounted, Bush the elder lost no time in a sending the U.S. military to help Kuwait.

President Bush whipped up support against Iraq by using the fake "hostage" claim. This is where the Tavistock Institute will fail: While it has been able to convince the majority of Americans that our policies for the Middle East are right, Tavistock has not been able to gain control of Syria, Iran, Iraq, Algeria and Saudi Arabia.

It is at this point that Tavistock's devious plan to dispossess the Arab nations of their oil is coming unglued. The days when MI6 could dispatch "Arabists" like the Philby's and Captain Hill to undermine Muslim states has long since gone.

The Arab countries have learned from their mistakes, and today, they trust the British Government far less than they did at the start of WWI. The dictatorship of Mubarak of Egypt is in trouble. Muslim fundamentalists seek to make tourism hazardous, and

Egypt relies on hard currency from abroad to keep floating besides the $3 billion annual gift from U.S. taxpayers. Likewise, Syria is not going to stand alongside U.S. policies that favor Israel over the Palestinians for very much longer.

At home, billions of dollars were poured into the coffers of Tavistock by the U.S. government: Among the beneficiaries of these billions of dollars were the National Training Laboratories, Harvard Psychological Clinic, Wharton School, Stanford's Hoover Institute, Rand, MIT, The National Institute of Mental Health, Georgetown University, Esalen Institute, Center for Advanced Study in Behavioral Sciences, Institute for Social Research at Michigan and scores of other think tanks and institutions of higher learning.

The task of setting up these affiliates in the U.S. in intelligence world wide was given to Kurt Lewin, who we have already met, but whose name was most probably not known to more than 100 people before my story about Tavistock broke. Yet this man and John Rawlings Reese did more to damage the institutions upon which the U.S. Republic rests, than anything Hitler or Stalin could have accomplished. The way in which Tavistock unraveled the warp and woof of our social fabric which holds the nation together, makes a chilling and frightening narrative of which the "normalizing" of homosexual and lesbian lifestyles is a small, but significant achievement; a far greater and more chilling achievement was the success of mass brainwashing through opinion polling.

Why do Reese's Tavistock techniques work so well in practice? Reese perfected his mass brainwashing experiments through stress tests, or psychological shocks, also known as stressful events. The Reese theory, now amply proved, was that if entire populations could be subjected to stress tests, then it would be possible first, to work out in advance, what mass population responses would be to given stress events.

In a very explicit way, this technique is at the heart of creating the desired public opinion through polling, which was used with devastating effect to shield the Clinton administration from the scandals swirling around the White House, and which now shields Bush the younger from being removed from the White House.

CHAPTER 26

How mediocre politicians, actors and singers are "puffed."

This technique is what is known as "profiling", and can be applied to individuals, small or large groups of people, mass groups of people and or organizations of all sizes. They are then "puffed" to become "stars." While still in his early twenties in Arkansas, William Clinton was profiled for acceptance in the Rhodes scholarship program. His progress was profiled throughout his career, and especially during the Vietnam War period. Then, after he proved himself, Clinton was "groomed" for the White House and then constantly "puffed."

The whole operation was under the control of the Tavistock Institute's brainwashers. This is the way these things work. Thus are the tools forged to literally make candidates, especially ones who are deemed suitable for public office; candidates who can always be counted on to do the "right" thing. Congress is full of them. Gingrich was a typical successful "Tavistock product" until his conduct was uncovered. Trent Lott, Dick Cheney, Charles Schumer, Barney Frank, Tom DeLay, Dennis Hastert, Dr. Frist, and so on are other examples of Tavistock "graduates." The same technique is applied to actors, singers, musicians and entertainers.

Heavy propaganda was used to convince the population that unwelcome "environmental social turbulences" were the result of the changing times in which we live, whereas, as we now know, special new-science scientists designed programs (stress programs) to artificially create "environmental social turbulences" and then pass them off as resulting from a natural condition, best known as "changing times."

Tavistock's new science scientists were confident that we would not apply the principle "for every effect there must be a cause"— and they were right. For instance we meekly accepted the "Beatles" and their "novel music" and lyrics-if one dare call it music and lyrics, having been told, that the group wrote it all themselves.

Actually Tavistock graduate Theo Adorno, whose 12-atonal discords were scientifically pitched to create mass "environmental social turbulences" all across America, wrote the music. None of the Beatles could read music. Nevertheless, they were "puffed" day and night without ceasing until everything about them, - lies and all, was accepted as truth.

Tavistock proved over and over again, that when a large group is successfully profiled, it can be subjected to "inner directional conditioning" in just about every aspect of social and political life.

An integral part of Tavistock's mass mind control experiments in the U.S., which have been going on since 1946, poll taking-opinion making has been by far it's most successful undertakings. America was whipsawed and did not know it.

Just to prove the success of his techniques, Reese got Tavistock to test a large group of people on a conspiracy- related subject. It turned out that 97.6 percent of those who were questioned utterly rejected the idea that an overall conspiracy exists. How much less then would our people believe that they have been under direct attack by Tavistock for the past 56 years? We have radio talk show hosts like Rush Limbaugh, who constantly tell audiences that there is no conspiracy.

How many people would believe that for the past 56 years,

Tavistock has been sending an invisible army of shock troops, into every hamlet, village, town and city across this nation? The task of the invisible army is to infiltrate, tamper with, and modify collective social behavior, by means of "inner directional conditioning."

The Reese "invisible army" is made up of real professionals who know their job and are dedicated to the task they were commissioned to do. They are found today in the halls of justice, police, churches, school boards, sports bodies, newspapers, television studios, government advisory boards, town councils, state legislatures, and are legion in Washington. They run for every office from county councilor to sheriff to judge, from school board member to city councilman, and even, for the office of the President of the United States of America. How this works was explained by John Rawlings Reese, back in 1954:

"Their job is to apply the advanced techniques of psychological warfare as we know them to whole population groups that will grow ever larger, so that whole populations may be more easily controlled. In a world driven completely mad, groups of Tavistock psychologists linked to each other, capable of influencing the political and governmental field must be arbiters, the power cabal."

Will this frank confession convince conspiracy skeptics? Probably not, as it is doubtful whether such closed minds could have any real knowledge of these things. Such information is wasted on radio "talking heads."

A director of the Reese invisible army was Ronald Lippert, whose specialty was tinkering with the minds of children.

Dr. Fred Emery was another of Tavistock's "linked psychologists" who was on the board of President Johnson's Kerner Commission.

Emery was what Tavistock called a "social environmental turbulence" specialist, the bottom line of which is that when a whole population group is subjected to social crises, it breaks down into synoptic idealism and finally fragments; that is to say, it just gives up trying to cope with the problem or problems.

The word "environmental" has nothing to do with ecology issues, but has to do with the particular environment into which the specialist has injected himself with the specific intent of making trouble—"turbulences" or "stress patterns."

This has already happened with rock and roll, drugs, free love (abortion), sodomy, lesbianism, pornography, street gangs, a constant attack on family life, on the institution of marriage, on social order, on the Constitution and especially on the 2nd and 10th Amendment.

Where this has happened, we find communities powerless to cope with a broken-down justice system, school boards teaching evolution, minors being encouraged to buy condoms and even "children's rights" being pushed. "Children's rights", usually mean children should be allowed to disobey their parents, a key issue in every Socialist's "child care" program. Members of the Reese Invisible Army are entrenched in the House and Senate, in the military, the police, and in virtually every government office in the land.

After studying the State of California, I came to the conclusion that it has the largest contingent of "Invisible Army" shock troops in the country, which has made California something very close to a socialist, police state. I believe California will be the "role model" for the rest of the nation.

At present there are no laws on the books that make this type of conditioning illegal. Reese and Lewin researched the laws of England and the United States and concluded that it was legal to "condition" a person without his or her consent or knowledge.

We need to change this. Polling is an integral part of "conditioning." Tavistock's "Invisible Army" of shock troops has changed the way America thinks about rock, premarital sex, drug taking, children born out of wedlock, promiscuity, marriage, divorce, family life, abortion, homosexuality and lesbianism, the Constitution and yes, even murder, not to mention that lack of morals is fine as long as one does a good job.

In the early years of Tavistock, the "Leaderless Group Concept" was used to lay the America we once knew, in the dust. In charge of the project was W.R. Bion, who ran the Wharton School of Economics for years, where such nonsense as free trade and Keynesian economics are taught. Japan stayed with the American model taught by General McArthur — not the Wharton School fraud—and look at Japan today. Don't blame the Japanese for their success - blame Tavistock for destroying our economic system. But Japan's turn is coming! No nation will be spared in the final onslaught to usher in a One World Government in a New World Order.

The "Brain Trust" in charge of Tavistock's War on America (1946--), consisted of Bernays, Lewin, Byron, Margaret Meade, Gregory Bateson, H.V. Dicks, Lippert, Nesbit and Eric Trist. Where did the "Invisible Army" shock troops get their training? They got it from Reese at Tavistock, from where they fanned out across America to sow their seeds of "environment social turbulence stress patterns."

They fanned out into every level of American society, obtaining posts in places where they could exert the influence they had been taught how to use by Reese. Decisions made by the members of the Invisible Army of shock troops have profoundly affected America at every level, and the worst is yet to come.

Just to give a few examples of who some the leading shock troops were, let's mention George Schultz, Alexander Haig, Larry King, Phil Donahue, Admiral Burkley (deeply involved in the cover-up of the Kennedy assassins), Richard Armitage, Billy Graham, William Paley, William Buckley, Pamela Harriman (since deceased,) Henry Kissinger, George Bush and the late Katherine Meyer Graham not to mention the caravan that arrived in Washington from Arkansas in 1992, headed by Mr. and Mrs. Clinton at whose hands the nation was soon to be torn apart. Newcomers include Rush Limbaugh, Bill O'Reilly, Larry King and Karl Rove.

Business leaders in shock troop groups are legion, far too many to list here. Thousands of such Invisible Army shock troops of the Business Brigade were turned out at Tavistock's U.S. facility, the National Training Laboratory (NTL), which began its existence on the huge, sprawling New York estate of Averill and Pamela Harriman. As we now know, Mrs. Harriman was the one who selected Clinton for special training and ultimately, the Oval Office.

At the National Training Laboratory corporate leaders were trained in stress situations and how to manage them. Companies who sent their top executives to NTC to receive for Tavistock training included Westinghouse, B.F. Goodrich, Alcoa, Halliburton, BP, Shell, Mobil-Exxon Eli Lily, DuPont, the New York Stock Exchange, Archer Daniels Midland, Shell Oil. Mobil Oil, Conoco, Nestle, AT&T, IBM and Microsoft. Worse yet, the U.S. government sent its top echelon personnel drawn from the U.S. Navy, the U.S. State Department, the Civil Service Commission, and the Air Force. Your tax dollars, by the million, paid for the "education" Tavistock gave these government employees at Arden House on the Harriman estate.

CHAPTER 27

The Tavistock formula that got the U.S. into WWII

Perhaps the most of important aspect of their training was how to use public polls to make public policy comply with what Tavistock goals said were desirable. This mind-altering technique is called "opinion polling."

The maladaptive responses made possible by Tavistock's wholesale profiling, and in which maladaptive responses Tavistock's "Invisible Army" worked to perfection in the Gulf War.

Instead of rebelling against dragging this nation into a war against a friendly country with whom we had no quarrel, a war that was waged without a proper Congressional declaration of war, we were "turned" in its favor. In short, we were badly misled without knowing it, due to the "long-range inner-directional conditioning" the American people had been undergoing since 1946.

Tavistock advised President Bush the elder to use the following simple formula which Reese and Lewin instructed Allen Dulles to use back in 1941 when Roosevelt was preparing to drag America into the Second World War:

> ➢ What is the state of the morale and its probable course in the targeted country? (This also applied to morale in the U.S.)
> ➢ What is the state of susceptibility in the U.S. to the idea

that war in the Persian Gulf is necessary?
- ➢ What techniques could be used to weaken opposition in the U.S. to war in the Persian Gulf?
- ➢ What kind of techniques in psychological warfare would succeed in undermining the morale of the Iraqi people? (It was here that Tavistock slipped up very badly.)

Once Bush committed himself to Prime Minister Thatcher's 1991 Gulf War on behalf of Queen Elizabeth and her BP oil company, Tavistock put together a team, which included psychologists, public opinion makers, led by the brazen liars at Hill and Knowlton, and a host of Tavistock profilers. Every single one of the speeches made by President Bush with the intention of promoting war against Iraq was crafted by multi-discipline teams of writers trained by Tavistock.

Top-secret information on how the Gulf War was propagated and how the American people were swung behind that nasty, corrupt war by President George Bush was given to a Congressional committee recently. The report said that at an early stage of the plan to take out Iraq, the Bush administration was advised that public support was paramount and that he did not have the American people behind him.

Rule one was to establish in the mind of the American people the "great need to protect Saudi oil fields threatened by an Iraqi invasion under the leadership of a madman." Thus, although it was known from the beginning that Iraq had no designs on Saudi oil fields, the National Security Agency (NSA) gave out false and misleading information to the effect that the Saudi oil fields were the ultimate target of Iraq. This was a total fabrication, but it was the key to success. The National Security Agency has never been punished for its lying conduct.

The report stated that an unprecedented amount of television coverage would be needed to swing public support behind the war. The Bush administration early on secured the full cooperation of the three major networks, ABC, CBS and NBC and later CNN. In later years a virtual propaganda station, Fox News (also known as Faux News) was added. The amount of Gulf War and related subjects coverage in 1990 by these stations was three times that of any subject covered in 1989, and once the war began; coverage was five times greater than any other story, including Tiananmen Square.

In 2003, Bush the younger, followed very closely the formula that had succeeded for his father, but with some additional adaptations. News mixed with fiction (see the section about H.G. Wells "War of the Worlds") became more fiction mixed with news and blatant lying was resorted to so that straight reporting became impossible to distinguish from news mixed with fiction.

One of the principal players in the coverage of the war was CNN, which contracted with the Bush administration to bring the Gulf War to American sitting rooms on a round-the-clock basis. As a result of the mass of favorable, slanted news, the deployment of troops to the Gulf was favorably received by about 90 percent of the American people. It was just another way to practice opinion-making polling on the American people, just another way to brainwash them.

National Security Agency (NSA) advisors told the Bush administration that from the very start, the public had to be persuaded to go along with his Gulf War plans. It was decided to create a parallel between Hitler and Saddam Hussein, with the words "Saddam Hussein must be stopped" repeated over and over again, followed by lie that the Iraqi President "is acting like Hitler."

Later a dire threat was added, that Iraq had the capability to strike at the U.S. with long-range weapons of mass destruction. It was the adaptation of Stalin's edict that to capture and enslave your own people, first terrorize them.

British Prime Minister Blair went even further. Speaking in Parliament, he told the British people that "Saddam Hussein" had the capability to strike Britain and could do so within 45 minutes. He went as far as to warn British tourists vacationing in Cyprus to return to Britain as soon as possible as British intelligence had learned that Iraq was preparing to launch a nuclear strike against the island. Blair made his announcement in the full knowledge that Iraq's nuclear weapons program had been completely destroyed in 1991.

The first Bush administration's "skill" in communicating the need for a war in the Gulf reached its height with the Hill and Knowlton fabricated "incubator" story tearfully told by the daughter of the ambassador of Kuwait to Washington. The Senate—and the entire country— swallowed this massive fraud.

It was Kaiser Wilhelm II "cutting off the arms of young Belgian children" all over again, and with even greater success. After the Hill and Knowlton "big lie," 77 percent of Americans surveyed said they approved of using U.S. troops against Iraq, even though 65 percent of those polled did know where Iraq was on the map.

All major polls found that Bush's sidestepping of the Constitution was approved, because those polled had no idea of what a constitutional declaration of war was, nor that it was mandatory. The role played by the U.N. added to the "communication skills" of the Bush administration, the report said.

The second Bush administration used the same Tavistock methods and once again the American people went along with the lies and distortions presented to them as fact. The war was vigorously promoted by Vice President Cheney who led a massive campaign to force public opinion onto the side of George Bush. No other Vice President in the history of the United States had ever taken such an active part in forcing the American people into a war with Iraq.

Cheney appeared on television 15 times in one month and adamantly declared that the Taliban was behind the attack on the World Trade Towers in New York and that the Taliban was under the control of President Hussein. "The fight against terrorism had to be taken to the "terrorists" in Iraq," Cheney said, "before they could strike at the U.S. again."

Cheney continued in the same vein long after his claim was proved absolutely false. Although the world's greatest authorities came forward to announce that Iraq had nothing to do with the 9/11 and that there were no Taliban fighters in Iraq, Cheney kept up his drumbeat of lies, until Hans Blix, the former U.N. chief weapons inspector cut him off, and the Central Intelligence Agency reported to the U.S. Senate that no connections had been discovered between Iraq and the Taliban and with 9/11.

In fact, said the CIA report, Hussein hated the Taliban and had driven them out of Iraq many years before. We publish this information in the hope that the American people will not be so gullible the next time their President wants to get them involved in a war. We would also like the American people to know that they are being grossly misled by a foreign "think tank" that constantly misleads them on a multitude of issues.

Let us examine some of the issues and let us hope that the American people will never be misled again by the skilled "communicators."

The American people have been grossly misled about five major wars, and that should be enough for any nation. But unfortunately, the nonstop bombing of Iraq and Serbia by U.S. - British aircraft showed that the American people had learned nothing from the Gulf War and how it was instigated, and how they were lied to and manipulated in an utterly reprehensible manner.

The second Gulf War was ample proof that Tavistock's methods still work, so much so that blatant lying was resorted to with the knowledge that even if discovered as lies, the Bush administration knew that their lies would just be shrugged off, because the American people were now thoroughly conditioned in a state of permanent "shell-shock," to display no concern over what was a very serious position for any nation to find itself in.

What can be done about the grip Tavistock and its many affiliated institutions have on the country, the Christian Right, the Congress, our intelligence agencies and the State Department, a grip that extends all the way to the President and to our top military brass? As I previously stated, the main problem is to be able to convince the broad mass of Americans that what is happening to them and the country, is not a case of "changing times" due to circumstances beyond their control, but a carefully contrived plot, a real menace to the future of all of us, and not just some "conspiracy" theory.

We can arouse the nation, but only if a concerted effort is made at the grassroots level. The solution to the problem lies in educating Americans and by unified action.

There is a great and compelling need to educate the millions of people as to what the secret manipulators are doing, and more importantly, just how, and why they are doing it. Urgent constitutional action is needed to bring this about. There are many leading citizens, who have the power and the financial means to start a grass roots campaign. What is not wanted, is a third political party.

A grass roots movement, properly educated and acting in concert is the only way (at least in my opinion) that we are going to win our country back from the dark and evil forces that have it by the throat. Together, in a grass roots movement, we can shake America free from the grip of foreign powers, powers the Tavistock Institute serves so well, foreign powers that are bent upon the destruction of America as constituted by our Founding

Fathers.

This work on the Tavistock Institute is another "first" in my series on major organizations whose names will be new to most readers. Tavistock is the most important nerve center in the U.S., and it has poisoned and gradually altered for the worse, every facet of our lives since 1946, when it began its North America operations.

Tavistock has played and is playing the leading role in shaping U.S. policies and world events. It is undoubtedly, the mother of all mind control and mind conditioning centers in the world. In the United States it has a great deal of control over day-to-day affairs and has a direct hand in the course and direction of such American think tanks as Stanford Research, Esalen Institute, Wharton School, MIT, the Hudson Institute, the Heritage Foundation, the Georgetown University and even more directly, extends its influence to the White House and the State Department. Tavistock has a profound influence in shaping U.S. domestic and foreign policy.

Tavistock is a study center devoted to the service of the Black Nobility and those devoted to promoting the New World Order inside a One World Government.

Tavistock does work for the Club of Rome, the CFR, Trilateral Commission, the German Marshall Fund, the Mont Pelerin Society, the Ditchley Group, the Quator Coronati Freemason control lodge and the Bank of International Settlements.

CHAPTER 28

How Tavistock makes well people sick

Tavistock's story begins with its founder, Brig. Gen. John Rawlings Reese in 1921. It was Reese who evolved Tavistock's methods of mass "brainwashing". Tavistock was founded as a research center for British Special Intelligence Service (SIS).

It was Reese who launched the method of controlling political campaigns, as well as mind control techniques, which continue to this very day, and it was Reese and Tavistock who taught the USSR, North Vietnam China and Vietnam how to apply his techniques—all they ever wanted to know about how to brain wash individuals or a mass of people.

Reese was a close confidant of the late Margaret Meade and her husband Gregory Bateson, both of whom played major roles in shaping U.S. institutions that make government policy. He was also a friend of Kurt Lewin, who was expelled from Germany after being accused of being an active Zionist. Lewin fled Germany when it became apparent that the NSDP would control Germany. Lewin rose to become Tavistock's director in 1932. He played a major role in preparing the American people for entry into WWII. Lewin was responsible for organizing the greatest propaganda machine known to mankind, which he directed against the whole German nation. Lewin's machine was responsible for whipping the American public opinion into favoring the war by engendering a climate of hatred against Germany. What was it that made the Reese method so successful? Basically, it was this: The same psychotherapy techniques used to cure a mentally sick individual could be applied in the opposite direction.

It could also used to make healthy people become mentally ill. Reese began his long series of experiments in the 1930s using British Army recruits as test cases. From there Reese progressed to perfecting mass brainwashing techniques, which he was later to apply to countries slated for change. One such country was the United States, which remains the focus of attention of Tavistock. Reese began applying his behavior modifications techniques against the American people in 1946. Few if any realized the extreme threat to America, which Reese posed.

The British Army Psychological Warfare Bureau was set up at Tavistock through secret agreements with Churchill, well before Churchill became prime minister. The agreements gave the British Special Operations Executive, commonly known as the SOE, full control over the policies of the U.S. Armed Forces, acting through civilian channels, and which invariably, became official U.S. Government policy.

That agreement is still firmly in place, as unacceptable to patriotic Americans today, as it was when established. It was the discovery of this agreement that led Gen. Eisenhower to issue his historical warning about powers accumulated in the hands of the "military industrial complex."

So that we fully understand the influence of Tavistock in the daily political, social, religious and economic life of the U.S., allow me to explain that it was Kurt Lewin, the second in command who was responsible for founding the following American institutions, many of whom were responsible for making profound changes in U.S. foreign and local policies:

> The Harvard Psychological Clinic

> The Massachusetts Institute of Technology (MIT)

> The Committee on National Morale

> ➢ Rand Corporation
> ➢ National Defense Resources Council
> ➢ The National Institute for Mental health
> ➢ The National Training Laboratories
> ➢ The Stanford Research Center
> ➢ The Wharton School of Economics.
> ➢ The New York Police Department
> ➢ The FBI
> ➢ The CIA
> ➢ The Rand Institute

To Lewin fell the task of selecting key personnel for these and other highly prestigious research institutions; including Esalen, the Rand Corporation; the United States Air Force, the Navy, the Joint Chiefs of Staff, and the State Department. In later years Tavistock conditioned those chosen to operate the ELF weather modifications facilities located in Wisconsin and Michigan, as a defense against those operated from the Kola Peninsula in Russia.

It was through institutions like Stanford and Rand that the treasonous, infamous "MK Ultra" project got its start. "MK Ultra" was a 20-year experiment utilizing LSD and other "mind-altering" drugs, carried forward under the direction of Aldous Huxley and the guru of the "Ban the Bomb" movement, Bertrand Russell (the senior statesman of the 300) for and on behalf of the CIA.

In the second Gulf War Tavistock-trained operatives showed U.S. General Miller how to run systematic torture to extract "information" from Muslim captives held at Abu Graib prison in Iraq and Guantanamo Bay in Cuba that shocked and disgusted the world when they were exposed. Through these and other similar mind control, mood-altering drugs, Lewin, Huxley and Russell were able to do indescribable damage to the youth of America, damage from which we, as a nation, will probably never fully recover. Their horrible drug experiments were carried out from Stanford Research, McGill University, and Bethesda Naval Hospital and at U.S. Army locations scattered all across the land.

It is worth repeating that the movement, which sprouted among our youth in the 1950s--1960s, known as the "New Age" and or the "Age of Aquarius", was a Tavistock program. There was noting spontaneous about it. Nudity was introduced in conformity with the course taken to demean women.

By 2005 the "new" fad is called "Hip-Hop" a type of dance game played mainly by children in the poorest suburbs of America's cities. It was picked up by Tavistock and turned into a full-blown industry with their specialists writing the "music and lyrics" until it is one of the best profit-makers for the recording industry.

Reese's methods were closely followed by Aldous Huxley, Bertrand Russell, Arnold Toynbee and Alistair Crowley. Russell was particularly adept at working Tavistock methods in forming his "CND": "Ban the Bomb" campaign which opposed U.S. nuclear experiments Tavistock "think tanks" received massive U.S. Government funding. Such institutions conduct research experiments with mass population conditioning. The CND movement was a front from behind which Huxley dispensed drugs for the youth of Britain.

In these experiments the American people have been more of a target than any other national group in the world. As I disclosed in 1969 and 2004, since 1946 the U.S. Government has poured billions of dollars into projects, which may be classed as "undercover operations", that is, the experimental programs go under other name and titles so that the unsuspecting American people raise no protest at such lavish government spending.

In such Tavistock experiments, every aspect of America's way of life, its customs, its traditions, its history, are examined to see if they can be subjected to change. Every aspect of our psychological and physiological life is constantly under scrutiny at Tavistock's U.S. institutions.

The "change agents" work tirelessly to change our way of life and make it look as such changes are merely "changing times" to which we must adapt. These forced changes are to be found in politics, religion, music, the way the news is manufactured and reported, the style of delivery of the news readers with the preponderance of American women readers who had every last trace of femininity driven out of them; the style and delivery of speeches made by Mr. Bush (short staccato sentences) accompanied by facial contortions and body movement taught by change artists, his manner of walking (U.S. Marine style), the rise of the so- called Christian fundamentalists in politics, the overwhelming support for "isms", the list is endless.

The outcome, the net result of these experimental programs determine how and where we shall live in the present and the future, how we will react to stressful situations in our national and personal life, and how our thinking on a national level regarding education, religion, morals, economics and politics can be channeled in the "right direction."

We, the People, have been and are being endlessly studied at Tavistock's Institutions. We are dissected, profiled, thought-read, and the data entered into computer data banks for the purposes of shaping and planning how we will react to planned future shocks and stressful situations. All this is done without our consent and in gross violation of our constitutional right to privacy.

These profiling results and prognostications are entered into data bases in computers at the National Security Agency, the FBI, the Department of Defense Intelligence Agency, and the Joint Chiefs of Staff, the Central Intelligence Agency, the National Security Agency to name but a few places where such data is stored.

The lines between internal and external spying are being blurred as the American people are conditioned for the coming One World Government wherein surveillance of individuals will reach unprecedented levels.

It was this kind of information which allowed the FBI to get away with burning David Koresh and his Branch Davidians, while the nation watched it happening on national television, without hardly a whimper of protest from the people and, an astonishing lack of protest from Congress. In one move, the States rights of Texas were destroyed. Waco was meant as a test case to see how the population would react to witnessing the 10th Amendment being destroyed before their very eyes, and, as profiled, the people of Texas and the United States acted precisely in the manner of the Tavistock profile; they acted like sheep peacefully grazing on grass as the Judas goat that would lead them to the slaughterhouse circled the flock.

What has happened, and is happening on an ongoing basis, was foretold by Carter's national Security Advisor, Zbigniew Brzezinski, in his New Age book, "The Technocratic Era" published in 1970. What he predicted is happening before our eyes, but the deadly sinister nature of these unfolding events is lost upon the people. The reality of what Brzezinski foretold in 1970 has come to pass. I suggest that you read the book—if it is obtainable—and then as I have done, compare events that have transpired since 1970 with what is stated in "The Technotronic Era." The accuracy of Brzezinski's forecasting is not only amazing, but also rather frightening.

If you are still skeptical, then read 1984 by George Orwell, a former M16 British intelligence operative. Orwell had to write his startling revelation as fiction to avoid being prosecuted under Britain's Official Secrets Act. Orwell's "newspeak" is now everywhere to be found, and just as he predicted, arouses no opposition.

Readers thought Orwell was describing Russia, but he was foretelling the coming of a regime far worse than the Bolshevik regime, the New World Order government of Great Britain.

One has only to look over the legislation passed by the Blair regime to see that liberties have been crushed, political dissent has been crushed, the Magna Carta put to flames and in its place, a set of draconian laws that makes for ominous reading. "As goes England today, so goes the United States tomorrow" according to an old saying.

Like it or not, Brzezinski predicted that We, the People, would have nothing left of our right to privacy; every little detail of our lives would be known by government, and subject to instant recall from data banks. By the year 2000, he said, private citizens would be in the grip of government control as never before experienced by any other nation.

Today, in 2005, we are under constant surveillance such as could not be imagined a few years ago, the Fourth Amendment has been trampled, our best protection from a gargantuan state, the 10th Amendment no longer in existence, and it has all been made possible through the work of Reese and the Social Sciences scientists who control the Tavistock Institute.

In 1969, by an order of the Committee of 300, Tavistock established the Club of Rome, as first reported in my monographs of 1969. The Club of Rome then established the North Atlantic Treaty Organization (NATO) as a political alliance.

By 1999, we were discovering the truth about NATO; it is a political entity with military support by its member-nations, Tavistock provided key personnel for NATO from its inception and it still does. They write all the key policies for NATO. In other words, Tavistock controls NATO.

Proof of this can be seen in the way in which NATO was able to bomb Serbia for 72 days and nights and get away with it, although it violated the four Geneva Conventions, the Hague Convention, the Nuremberg Protocols, and the United Nations charter. There was no outcry from the American people or the British people against such barbarous action.

Of course this had all been predetermined from Tavistock's data banks: They knew exactly how the public would react or not react to the bombing. Had an unfavorable determination been made beforehand as to how the public would react, there would have been no bombing raids over Serbia.

Precisely the same Tavistock studies were used to ascertain public reaction to raining down cruise missiles and bombs on the open city of Baghdad in 2002, Rumsfeld's infamous "shock and awe" tactic. Barbarous behavior of this magnitude was indulged in because the President and his men already knew beforehand that there would be no outcry from the American public.

Both the Club of Rome and NATO have considerable influence in foreign policy decisions taken by the U.S. Government, and they continue to do so, today, as we saw in the case of the unprovoked attack on Serbia and Iraq acceded to by the Clinton and Bush administrations, respectively. History provides other examples of national control of the U.S. by Tavistock.

When the Second World War broke out, the United States was subjected to a preplanned brainwashing campaign of the most massive proportions, prepared and executed by the Tavistock Institute.

This would pave the way for a smooth entry of the U.S. into a war that was none of our business and muzzle those opposed to it. All of Roosevelt's grand speeches were composed by technicians skilled in mind control at Tavistock, many of them emanating from the Fabian Society.

Americans were told that the war was started by Germany; that the danger of Germany to world peace was far greater than the threat of Bolshevism would ever be. A substantial number of socials scientists working at Tavistock's U.S. institutions were selected to lead the charge in persuading the American people that America's entry into the war was the proper course for it to take. However, they did not succeed until Japan was "forced to fire the first shot" at Pearl Harbor.

CHAPTER 29

Topological psychology gets the U.S. into the War in Iraq

Kurt Lewin's topological psychology—standard fare at Tavistock institutions—was taught to selected American scientists sent there to learn its methodology, and the group returned to the U.S. to spear-head the drive to force Americans to believe that support for Britain—the instigator of the war— was in our best interests. Topological psychology is still the most advanced method of inducing behavior modifications, whether in individuals or in mass population groups.

Unhappily, topological psychology was used all too successfully by the mass media in rushing America into a British-contrived situation in Iraq, another war in which we had no business involving ourselves. The professional liars who run this country, the whores of the media, the treasonous, treacherous "spokesmen" for the One World Government—New World Order, used exact topological psychology against those who said we should not be attacking Iraq.

Bush, Baker, Haig, Rumsfeld, Rice, Powell, General Myers, Cheney and those in Congress who fawned all over them in a servile display of bootlicking—brainwashed the American people to believe that Pres. Saddam Hussein of Iraq was a monster, an evil man, a dictator, a threat to world peace, who had to be removed from power, even though Iraq had never done anything to harm the United States. While there may have been some truth to the allegations that Hussein had done some terrible deeds, the same could be said of Wilson and Roosevelt magnified a million times.

Tavistock's war on the U.S. Constitution had completely dumbed-down the American people to where they somehow believed that the U.S. had the right to attack Iraq and remove its leader, even though the Constitution expressly forbids such action not to mention that it violated international law and the Nuremberg Protocols. As already stated, it takes a "contrived situation" to get the American people fired up.

In WWI it was the "atrocities" committed by the Kaiser. In WWII it was Pearl Harbor, in Korea it was the "ghost torpedo boats" of North Korea's attack on the U.S. Navy that never happened.

In Iraq it was the deceit and lies of April Glaspie; in Serbia, it was the "concern" of Madame Albright for the alleged "persecution" of Albanian illegal aliens flooding into Serbia to escape the economic misery of their homeland that was the excuse for her self-righteous crusade against Serbia.

Tavistock coined a new name for the illegal Albanians; henceforth they were to be called "Kosovars." Of course the profiled and programmed American public made no objection when Serbia, without just cause and without ever having harmed the United States, was mercilessly bombed for seventy-six days and nights!

The real danger to peace comes from our one-sided policy toward Middle East nations, and our attitude toward Socialist governments. Appeals to rally around the flag in the early stages of WWII were pure Reese topological psychology— and it was repeated in the Gulf War, the Korean War, Iraq (twice) and Serbia.

Soon it will be North Korea again. The U.S. has persecuted that nation for more than 25 years-only this time the excuse will be that North Korea is about to drop a nuclear bomb on an American city! In all these wars, the American people succumbed to the big drum of Tavistock brainwashing under the guise of "patriotism" tinged with a heavy dose of fear, banged night and day. Americans believed the myth that Germany was the "bad guy" bent upon ruling the world; we rejected the threat of Bolshevism.

Twice we were whipped into frenzy against Germany. We believed our controllers because we did not know that we were brainwashed, manipulated and controlled. And so our sons were shipped off to die on Europe's battlefields for a cause, which was not America's cause.

Immediately after Winston Churchill became Britain's Prime Minister after he ousted Neville Chamberlain because he had succeeded in making a peace agreement with Germany; Churchill the great paragon of belief in respect for international law began breaking international laws that governed civilized conduct during wars.

Acting on the advice of Tavistock theoretician Richard Crossman—Winston Churchill adopted Tavistock's plan for terror bombing of civilian population. (We were to see the same policy being carried out in Iraq and Serbia.)

Churchill gave the Royal Air Force (RAF) orders to bomb the small German city of Freiberg, an undefended city, one on the list of such cities in Germany and Britain, which both sides had agreed in a written pact was an "open, undefended city" not to be bombed.

On Saturday afternoon, February 27 1940, a raid on Freiberg was carried out by RAF "Mosquito" bombers, killing 300 civilians including 27 children at play in a schoolyard, plainly visible as a school.

This was the start of the RAF's terror bombing campaign against German civilian targets; the infamous Tavistock-inspired

Prudential Bombing Survey, which was directed solely against German worker housing and the civilian infrastructure. Tavistock assured Churchill that such mass terror bombing would bring Germany to its knees once the target of destroying 65% of German worker housing was reached.

Churchill's decision to launch terror bombing against Germany was a war crime and remains a war crime. Churchill was a war criminal and should have been put on trial for his hideous crimes against humanity.

The bombing of Freiberg Germany, without consultation with France, was the first departure from civilized conduct in WWII and the British Government was solely to blame for the air raids by the Germans, which followed. Churchill's terror tactics were followed to the letter by the U.S. in the undeclared war against Iraq, Serbia, Iraq again and Afghanistan, which began in March of 1999, in the same vein of no mercy as displayed by Churchill.

Kurt Lewin, whose hatred of Germany knew no bounds, developed the policy of terror bombing of civilian housing. Lewin was the "father" of the Strategic Bombing Survey, deliberately designed to destroy 65 percent of German worker housing and kill in an indiscriminate manner, as many German civilians as possible.

German military casualties were far exceeded by civilian casualties of the war, as a result of "Bomber" Harris and his heavy bomber night raids by the RAF on German worker housing. This was a major war crime that has still gone unpunished.

This gives the lie to the propaganda put out by Tavistock that Germany began such terror raids. The facts are that it was only after eight weeks of terror-raids on Berlin had caused heavy damage to civilian housing and non-military targets had taken thousands of civilian lives that the Luftwaffe retaliated by attacks on London. German retaliation came only after countless appeals by Hitler, directly to Churchill to stop breaking their agreement, which the "great man" ignored.

Churchill, the master liar, the consummate liar, with the help of, and under the direction of Lewin was able to persuade the world that Germany started civilian bombing as a deliberate policy when, as we have seen, it was Churchill who initiated it. British War Office and RAF documents reflect this position. The damage done to London by the Luftwaffe was relatively mild when compared with what the RAF did to German cities, but the world never heard about that.

The world saw only what amounted to small sections of London damaged by German air raids with Churchill striding over the rubble, his jaw jutting out and a cigar clenched between his teeth, the epitome of defiance! How well Tavistock had taught him to stage such events! (We see the echo of Churchill's affected mannerisms appearing in George Bush who appears to have undergone some "training" of his own.)

Churchill's "bulldog" character was created by Tavistock. His true character was never revealed. The callous bombing of Freiberg paled into a shadow compared with the callous, barbaric, un-Christian, inhuman fire-bombing of the open, undefended city of Dresden that took more lives than the subsequent atomic bomb attack on Hiroshima.

The bombing of Dresden and the timing of the raid was a cold-blooded decision taken in consultation with Tavistock by the "great man" to cause "shock and awe" and impress his friend, Joseph Stalin. It was also an outright attack on Christianity, timed to take place during Lent.

There was no reason military or strategic reason to fire bomb Dresden, which was selected as a target by Lewin. In my view, the fire bombing of Dresden, crowded with German civilian refugees fleeing from the Russian onslaught from the East, when Lent celebrations were being observed, ranks as the most heinous war crime ever committed. Yet, because the British and American people had been thoroughly programmed, conditioned and thoroughly brainwashed, hardly a murmur of protest was heard. The war criminals, "Bomber" Harris, Churchill, Lewin and Roosevelt, got away with this terrible crime against humanity.

On May 5, 2005, during a State visit to Berlin, Russian President Vladimir Putin held a joint conference with Germany Chancellor Gerhard Schroeder told the German newspaper Beeld that Allied forces cannot be absolved for the horrors of WWII, and that included the bombing of Dresden: "The Western allies didn't abound with any special humanity," he said. "It is incomprehensible to me to this day why Dresden was destroyed. There was no military reason for it."

Perhaps the Russian leader did not know about Tavistock and its Prudential Bombing Survey that ordained the terrible bombing, but certainly, readers of this work will now know why the barbaric and horrible atrocity was carried out.

To return to Reese and his early work at Tavistock involving brainwashing experiments on 80,000 British Army troops. After a five-year "re-programming" of these men, Reese was confident that his system of making mentally stable people ill, would work on any mass group. Reese was sure that he could give "treatment" to mass groups of people, whether it was desired by them or not, and without the victims even being aware of what was being done to their minds. When questioned about the propriety of his actions, Reese responded that it was unnecessary to first obtain permission from the "subjects" before commencing with his experiments.

The modus operandi developed by Reese and his gurus, proved to be successful. The Reese-Lewin method of tampering with minds proved highly effective and is still in wide use in America today, in 2005. We are tampered with, our opinions manufactured for us, all without our permission. What was the purpose of these behavior modifications? It was to bring about forced changes to our way of life, without our agreement and without even being aware of what is happening.

From his brightest students, Reese selected what he called "my first team" to become the first level of his "invisible college graduates" "shock troops" that were to be placed in key positions inside British Intelligence, the Army, Parliament and later, inside the Supreme Headquarters Allied Expeditionary Forces (SHAEF).

The "first team graduates" went on to fully control General Eisenhower, who became no more than a puppet in their hands. "First team graduates" were insinuated into every policy making body in the United States.

The "first team graduates" made U.S. policy decisions. The "Secret Team" as they were to become known, was responsible for the public execution of President. John F. Kennedy, in full view of America and the world as a lesson to future Presidents that they were to obey all directives received from the "Olympians". Kissinger was one of many "first team graduates" placed in a position of authority inside the U.S. Government, in the O.S.S. and the FBI.

A Canadian citizen, Major Louis Mortimer Bloomfield ran Division Five counterintelligence of the FBI during WWII. In Britain, it was H.V. Dicks who was responsible for placing "first team graduates" in key intelligence positions, the Church of England, the Foreign Office and the War Office, not to mention the Parliament.

Tavistock was able to conduct wartime experiments in peacetime, given all of the facilities made available to it, and with this experience, could tighten its grip on the U.S. and British military establishments and intelligence services.

In America, Tavistock's sinister experiments changed the American way of life, completely and forever. When this truth is recognized by the majority of our people, when the far-reaching control of Tavistock exercises over our daily lives is comprehended, only then will we be able to fight back, if indeed we have not by then become total shell-shocked automons.

By 1942 the command structure of British and U.S. military and intelligence services had become so enmeshed that they could no longer be separated or distinguished from each other.

This gave rise to the many weird and strange policies followed by our government, most of which policies directly contradicted the U.S. Constitution and the Bill of Rights and ran contrary to the wishes of We, the People, as expressed through our elected representatives in the Congress. In short, our elected representatives had lost control of our government. Winston Churchill called it "a special relationship."

At the close of WWII, a number of carefully selected and profiled senior political and military figures from Britain and the United States were invited to attend a conference chaired by Reese. What Reese told the group is taken from confidential notes compiled by one of those who attended the meeting but who has asked to remain anonymous:

"If we propose to come out in the open and attack national, social problems of our day, then we must have shock troops, and these cannot be provided by psychiatry based wholly on institutions.

We must have mobile teams of psychiatrists who are free to move around and make contact with local situation in particular areas. In a world driven completely mad, groups of psychiatrists linked to each other, each capable of influencing the entire field of politics and government must be the arbiters, the power cabal."

Could anything be clearer? Here was Reese advocating lawless conduct by a group of psychiatrists linked together to make up first teams for his invisible colleges, free from all social, ethical, and legal restraints, who could be moved to areas of mentally well population groups, which in the opinion of Reese and his team, needed to be made ill by reverse psychology "treatment". Being "well" included any community that had successfully resisted mass brainwashing, as the results of "polling" showed.

"First teams" would be followed by "shock troops" such as we see among the environmentalist groups. And this is not surprising as the Environmental Protection Agency (EPA) is a monster created by Tavistock's "environmental concerns," which concerns were generated by Tavistock themselves and passed on to the Environmental Protective Agency via shock troops.

The EPA is not the only Tavistock-generated creature. Abortion and homosexuality are Tavistock created and supported aberrations.

Because of Tavistock-created and supported programs, we in the United States have suffered a terrible degradation of our moral life, our religious life; debasement of music through the aberration of rock and roll "music," which became progressively worse following a relatively tame introduction by The Beatles followed by Rap and Hip-Hop; destruction of art, as we see pushed by PBS in the Mapplethorpe degenerate objects of derision. We have seen a proliferation of the drug culture and an intensified worship of the Golden Calf. The lust for money has never been higher in any civilization than the current one.

These are the bitter fruits of Tavistock policies implanted in our society by "invisible college graduates", who became school board members and insinuated themselves into leadership roles in our churches. They also insinuated themselves into important party political positions, at city and State levels, wherever their influence would be felt.

The "graduates" became members of labor mediation boards, school boards, university boards, trade unions, the military, the church, the communications media, the entertainment media and the civil service; as well as the Congress, to the extent where it becomes obvious to the trained observer that Tavistock has taken over the reins of government.

Reese and his Tavistock colleagues succeeded beyond their wildest dreams, having captured control of the major institutions upon which government rests. The parent, - the Committee of 300—must be delighted with the progress made by the young infant Club of Rome.

The Fourth of July has been rendered meaningless. There is no longer any American "independence" to celebrate. The victories of 1776 have been negated, largely reversed, and it remains only a matter of time before the U.S. Constitution is discarded in favor of a New World Order. In the tenure of G.W. Bush, we see that process accelerated.

CHAPTER 30

My choice of candidate, not my choice

Let us look at the way in which an election is run. The American people do not vote for a president. They vote for a party candidate chosen by the elect of the party, more often than not, entirely under the control of the Committee of 300. This is not a vote for a candidate of choice, as we are so often told. In truth, voters have no choice other than selecting from pre-chosen candidates.

The candidates the pubic think it is voting for by choice (our choice) have been thoroughly vetted by the Tavistock Institute, and we were then brainwashed into thinking of them in a virtuous manner.

Such impressions or sound bites are created in the studious of think tanks like Yankelovich, Skalley and White, run by Tavistock graduate Daniel Yankelovich. Tavistock-controlled "think tanks" tell us how to vote in their chosen manner. Since the advent of Yankelovich, the number of profiling" industries has proliferated to over one hundred and fifty such institutions. Take the examples of James Earl Carter, and George Bush. Carter came from relative obscurity to "win" the White House, which the media moguls said, proved that the U.S. system works.

In fact, what Carter's election proved was that Tavistock rules this country and can sway the majority of voters to vote for a man about whom they know almost nothing. Saying that "the system worked" in relation to Carter, and later, in relation to William Jefferson Clinton, was exactly the maladaptive response Tavistock expected from a mass-brainwashed populace.

What Carter mirrored was that voters will vote for a candidate pre-selected for them. No thinking person would have wanted Skull and Bones man George Bush as Vice President, yet Bush is what we got. How did it come about that Carter was able to reach the White House? It happened thusly: A certain Dr. Peter Bourne, Tavistock's in-house social psychologist was given the task of finding a candidate Tavistock could manipulate. In other words, Bourne was to find the "right" candidate for the job according to Tavistock's rule, one that could be sold to the voters.

Bourne, knowing Carter's history, put forward his name for consideration. Once Carter's record was approved, American voters were given "the treatment," that is to say; they were subjected to a sustained brainwashing campaign to persuade them that they had found Carter as their choice. In fact, by the time Tavistock was finished with the job, it was not really necessary to hold an election. It became a mere formality. Carter's victory was a personal victory for Reese, while Bush was a victory for Tavistock's methodology. An even greater "success story" was to follow in the selling of William Jefferson Clinton as a candidate for the White House, a feat which might have been impossible in any other country.

Then came the selling of George W. Bush, a failed businessman and one who had sidestepped serving in Vietnam and a man with very thin experience.

Tavistock had to go into high gear, but even that was not enough. When it was certain that Bush was not going to win, the U.S. Supreme Court illegally intervened in a STATE election and awarded the prize to the loser.

A stupefied (shell-shocked) electorate let the enormous violation of the U.S. Constitution go unchallenged thereby assuring their future will be lived in a New World Order - International Communist One World Government International Communists dictatorship.

Reese continued to expand Tavistock's base of operations, taking on board Dorwin Cartwright, a highly skilled population profiler. One of his specialties was measuring population reaction to a food shortage. The object was to gain experience when the food weapon is brought into play against a population group unwilling to conform to Tavistock regulations.

Tavistock has planned it this way: The international food cartels will corner food production and distribution of the world's food resources. Famine is a weapon of war, just as weather modifications is a weapon of war. Tavistock will use the famine weapon without restraint, when the time is right. Continuing with the expansion of Tavistock, Reese recruited Ronald Lippert.

What Tavistock had in mind when it hired Lippert, was to get a foothold in the future control of education, starting with young children. Lippert was an expert in tinkering with the minds of the very young. An ex-O.S.S. operative, he was highly skilled theoretician, and a specialist in race mixing as a way of weakening national boundaries. Once installed at Tavistock, Lippert began his work by establishing a "think tank" devoted to what he called, "community interrelations," which involved seeking methods whereby natural race barriers might be dismantled.

The so-called "civil rights" legislation is pure Reese and Lippert, and has no constitutional basis in fact. (See "What you Should Know About The U.S. Constitution for a full explanation on so-called "civil rights.")

In passing I should say that all civil rights legislation in the U.S is predicated on the 14th Amendment, but the problem is that the fourteenth was never ratified. Thus it is not a part of the U.S. Constitution and all laws predicated upon it are null and void. In essence there is no such constitutional provision for civil rights.

Lippert established the rationale for Martin Luther King's "civil rights" over the fact that no basis for it existed in the Federal Constitution. Busing children past their schools was another Lippert-Reese brainwashing success. Busing children past their destination was certainly not a "right." To sell the idea of "civil rights" to the American populace at large, three "think tanks" were established:

➢ The Science Policy Research Center
➢ The Institute for Social Research
➢ The National Training Laboratories

Through the Science Policy Research Unit, Lippert was able to place thousands of his brainwashed "graduates" in key positions throughout the United States, West European (including Britain), France and Italy. Today, Britain, France, Italy and Germany all have Socialist governments, the groundwork for which was prepared by Tavistock.

Hundreds of upper-level executives from some of America's most prestigious corporations were trained at one or another of Lippert's institutions. The National Training Laboratories gained control of the 2-million strong National Education Association and with this success, came complete control over education in American schools and universities.

But perhaps the most profound influence exerted on America came with Tavistock's control of NASA, partially because of the Special Report on NASA's space program, written by Dr. Anatole Rappaport for the Club of Rome. The startling report was released at a seminar in May of 1967 to which only the most carefully selected and profiled delegates from the top echelons of business and governments of the most highly industrialized nations were invited.

Among the attendees were members of the Foreign Policy Institute, while the State Department sent Age of Aquarius conspirator, Zbigniew Brzezinski as its observer. In its final report, the Tavistock-controlled symposium derided NASA's work as "inappropriate" and suggested that its space programs be halted immediately. The U.S. Government duly obliged by cutting off funding, which caused NASA to lie dormant for 9 years—enough time for the Soviet space program to catch-up and forge ahead of the U.S. The United States has never been able to close the gap.

Rappaport's Special NASA Report stated that the agency was producing "too many skilled people; too many scientists and engineers," whose services would not be needed in the smaller, more beautiful post industrial society, mandated by the Club of Rome. Rappaport called our highly skilled and trained space scientists and engineers, "redundant." The U.S. Government, which I have already indicated appears to be under the thumb of Tavistock, thereupon cut funding. Interference with NASA is a perfect example of how Britain controls U.S. domestic and foreign policies.

Jewel in Tavistock's crown is the Aspen Institute of Colorado, which for years was under the direction of Robert Anderson, a graduate of the University of Chicago, preeminent for brainwashing in the United States. The Aspen facility is the North American home of the Club of Rome teaches that a return of the monarchy would be very good for America. John Nesbitt, another Tavistock graduate held seminars on a fairly regular basis at Aspen at which instituting a monarchy was promoted among top businessmen.

One of Nesbitt's students was William Jefferson Clinton, already then favored as presidential material. Nesbitt, like Anderson, is dazzled by British royalty and follows their Cathari doctrines of bogus concerns for ecology.

The Philosophical Radicals had introduced the Bogomils and Catharists beliefs into Socialist circles in Britain. Anderson's proteges were Margaret Thatcher and George Bush whose actions in the Gulf War showed that Tavistock had done its homework rather well. Anderson is typical of the duped, brainwashed "graduate leaders" and his specialty is teaching targeted groups of business leaders in environmental training.

Ecology issues are Anderson's forte. Although Anderson funds some of his activities from his own huge financial resources, he also receives donations from around the world, including donations from Queen Elizabeth and her consort, Prince Philip. Anderson founded the militant "Friends of the Earth" ecology movement and the "United Nations Conference on the Environment."

Aside from his Aspen activities, Anderson is president and CEO of the Atlantic Richfield Company—ARCO, on whose board of directors is to be found the following notables:

Jack Conway

He is best remembered for his work for the United Way Appeal Fund and as a director of the Socialist International Ford Foundation, both about as un-American as it is possible to get. Conway is also a director of the "Center for Change," a specialist Tavistock shock troops clearing house.

Philip Hawley

He is chairman of the Los Angeles Company, "Hawley and Hale," which interfaces with "Transamerica," a company specializing in making anti Christian, anti-family, pro- abortion, pro-lesbian, pro-homosexual, pro-drug movies. Hawley is associated with Bank of America, which funds the Center for the Study of Democratic Institutions, a classic Tavistock brainwashing institution think-tank for the promotion of drug usage and legalization of drugs.

Dr. Joel Fort

This British national, Fort was on the board of directors of the London "Observer" newspaper along with the Honorable David Astor and Sir Mark Turner, a director of the Royal Institute for Inter-national Affairs (RIIA), whose abject American servant is Henry Kissinger.

The Royal Institute of International Affairs (RIIA)

Founded the Council on Foreign Relations (CFR) as a sister organization, America's de- facto mid-level secret government, is the executive arm of the Committee of 300. In May of 1982, Kissinger proudly announced Tavistock's control of America.

The occasion was a dinner for RIIA members. Kissinger lauded the British Government as is expected of a Tavistock graduate. In his best gravel-voiced manner Kissinger said: "In my White House days, I kept the British Foreign Office better informed than I did the U.S. State Department."

The common denominator between the three Lippert institutions is the brainwashing methodology originally taught at Tavistock. All three of Lippert's institutes were funded by government grants. At these institutions, the top administrators and policy makers of the government were and are trained how to undermine America's established way of life, founded on Western civilization and upon the United States Constitution. The intent is to weaken and eventually break down the institutions that make up the foundation of the United States.

The National Education Association

An indication of just how great was Lippert's control of the National Education Association can be gauged from the en- bloc vote cast for William Jefferson Clinton by its brainwashed member-teachers, in accordance with the leadership's instructions.

The Corning Group

The company donated Wye Plantation to the Aspen Institute, which became the principal training ground for New Age recruits and "shock troops." James Houghton, Coming's Vice Chairman, is a messenger for the Pierepoint Morgan family of Morgan Guarantee and Trust on Wall Street. Morgan receives daily briefings from the RIIA directly from London, which briefings become INSTRUCTIONS to be conveyed to the U.S. Secretary of State.

Former Secretary of the Treasury William Fowler was part of Corning-Aspen interface. He is the chief proponent for handing over U.S. fiscal policies to the International Monetary Fund (IMF) and constantly pushed for the Bank of International Settlements to control internal U.S. banking. It is significant that Wye Plantation was the site of the Arab— Israeli peace talks known as the Wye Accords.

Executive Conference Center

Charged with teaching behavior modifications under the direction of Robert L. Schwartz, this "specialist training center" is run along the lines of the Esalen Institute.

Schwartz spent 3 years at Esalen Institute and worked closely with Aldous Huxley, Tavistock's No. I "respectable" drug culture pusher who was responsible for introducing LSD to American college students. Schwartz was also a close friend of anthropologist Margaret Meade and her husband, Gregory Bateson. From Stanford and Esalen, Schwartz moved to Terrytown House, the Mary Biddle Duke property in Westchester, where with huge grants from IBM and AT&T, opened the Executive Conference Center; the first full-time Age of Aquarius-New Age "graduate school" for top-flight corporate executives drawn from every spectrum of corporate America, industry, trade and banking.

Thousands of upper level executives and managers from corporate America, especially from Fortune 500 companies, the creme-del-le-creme of the business world, paid $750 per head to obtain instruction in Age of Aquarius Age methodology through seminars conducted by Schwartz, Meade, Bateson, and other Tavistock brainwashing specialists.

Schwartz was at one time strongly allied with Scientology, and he was also an editor of TIME magazine. Aspen Institute - New Age centers were generously funded by IBM and AT&T.

It is difficult for Americans who do not have access to this kind of information to believe that IBM and AT&T, two household names in Corporate America, would have anything to do with mind control, brainwashing, behavior modification and transcendental meditation; Bahai sensitivity training, Zen Buddhism, reverse psychology, and all of the other New Age - Age of Aquarius programs designed to break down the morals of the American people and weaken family life. Christianity was not taught.

Doubts would arise in the minds of most Americans who do not know the extent to which Corporate America rules the roost at home and abroad, in a manner dangerous to the U.S. Constitution and the Bill of Rights. Without Corporate America, we would never have suffered the Vietnam War, the Gulf War, war on Serbia, and a second war against Iraq. Nor would Carter and Clinton have had a ghost of a chance of sitting in the White House, against all odds!

If what is written here is not accurate, these companies could always deny its truths, but thus far, they have not done so. It would come as a shock to find that a large number of corporate giants that are household names to the American public, send their executives and upper level management personnel to have their brains scrambled by Schwartz, Meade, Bateson, John Nesbitt, Lewin, Cartwright and other Tavistock behavioral modifications and mind control specialists: At the Executive Conference Center, corporate executives meet with John Nesbitt, who owes his allegiance to the Black Nobility and the House of Guelph, better known as the House of Windsor; the RIIA, the Milner - Round Table Groups, the Club of Rome and Aspen Institute. Nesbitt is typical of the operatives used by the British Government to direct U.S. and foreign policies.

Nesbitt is a staunch monarchist and a Club of Rome specialist in zero growth for industry, especially heavy industry. He believes in zero growth post industrialism to the point of returning the world to a feudal state. At one of his brainwashing sessions, he told the executives from "Business America" (my new term):

"The United States is moving toward as monarchy just like Britain and a governing system in which Congress, the White House and the Supreme Court will be merely symbolic and ritualistic. This will constitute true democracy; the American people do not care who is President; half of them don't vote, anyway. America's economy is growing away from that of a nation-state and towards smaller and smaller power centers, possibly into multiple nations. We must substitute for the national state, a geographical, ecological state of mind."

"The United States will move away from a concentration of heavy industrial activity. Auto, steel, housing will never revive again. Buffalo, Cleveland, Detroit, the old industrial centers will die. We are moving toward an information society. There is and will continue to be a lot of pain, but on the whole, this economy is better off than it was a decade ago." Nesbitt was actually echoing the very sentiments expressed by Count Davignon in 1982.

CHAPTER 31

Zero Growth in Agriculture and Industry: America's Post Industrial Society.

In 1983 I wrote a monograph entitled, "The Death of the Steel Industry" in which I provided details of how French aristocrat Etienne Davignon of the Club of Rome was given the task of downsizing the American steel industry.

At the time this work was published, a lot of people were skeptical, but based upon information about the Club of Rome— which most Americans and most writers had never even heard of prior to my 1970 article of the same title; I felt sure, that Nesbitt's prediction could happen, and in the next seven years, it turned out to be accurate, although not in all ways. Although parts of Nesbitt's predictions were off—their time had not yet come - in many ways, he was correct, in so far as the intentions of our secret government go.

None of the captains of industry, who attended Tavistock's EEC brainwashing sessions, saw fit to protest what Nesbitt was saying. That being the case how could I expect that an unknown writer like myself, nobody had ever heard of, would make an impact?

The executive conferences and training sessions at Tarrytown House proved that Reese's brainwashing techniques were flawless. Here was a forum attended by the captains of industry, the elite of America's corporate world, quite happy to be participating in the demise of America's steel industry, sacrificing its unique domestic market that had made America a great industrial nation, tearing up the Constitution and the Bill of Rights and embracing genocidal programs calling for the culling of half of the world's population; substituting Eastern mysticism and the Kabala for Christianity; applauding programs that would result in a breakdown of the morals of the nation and destruction of family life; a future Balkanized America.

No one could deny, looking at the state of America today in 2005, that Reese and his Tavistock methods did an astonishing job in brainwashing the leaders of our corporate world, our political and religious leaders, our judges and our educators, and the guardians of the morals of the nation, not to mention the U.S. House of Representatives and the Senate.

In 1974, Professor Harold Isaacson of the Massachusetts Institute of Technology (MIT) in his book, "Idols of the Tribe," laid bare Tavistock's blueprint to combine Mexico, Canada and the U.S. into Balkan-type states. I would remind my readers that MIT was founded by Kurt Lewin, the same Kurt Lewin who was forced out of Germany because of his brainwashing experiments; the same Lewin who planned the Strategic Bombing Survey; Reese's number one theoretician.

All that Isaacson did was to spell out the Aquarian blueprint in a more readable, detailed manner than the Stanford-Willis Harmon Aquarian study. In 1981, seven years later, Isaacson's ideas (Tavistock's Aquarian blueprint) were presented to the public by Joel Gallo, editor of the Washington Post, and the mouthpiece of Britain's House of Windsor and the Club of Rome. Gallo called his presentation, The Nine Nations of North America. Gallo's version of Tavistock's blueprint for a future America envisaged:

> ➤ The death of the steel industry and a decline of industry in the industrial Northeast and the founding of the "Nation of the North East."
> ➤ Dixie, the Emerging Nation of the South.

> ➤ Etopia, consisting of the coastal fringes of the Northwest Pacific.

> ➤ (Willis Harmon in his Age of Aquarius paper used the term, "ecotopia.")

> ➤ The balance of southwest America to be combined with Mexico as a "breadbasket" region.

> ➤ The Midwest to be designated "The Empty Quarter."

> ➤ Parts of Canada and the islands to be designated "For Special Purposes"

(Perhaps these territories will be the sites for future "Gulags," now that we have seen the unthinkable-the Guantanamo Bay prison reconstruction facility where mind tinkering and torture are in actual practice.)

In all these latter areas there would be nothing in the way of large cities, conflicting with "ecotopia". Just to make sure that everybody understood that they knew what he was talking about, Gallo presented a map with his book. The problem is that the American people did not take Gallo seriously. It was precisely the way Tavistock expected them to react in what it called a "perfect maladaptive response."

The American right wing grew up on the Rockefeller, Warburgs, Freemasonry, the Illuminati, Council on Foreign Relations, the Federal Reserve conspiracy, and the Trilateral Commission. Nothing very much of the inner core workings had been published.

When I began to publish my research in 1969, the American people mostly had not heard of the Committee of 300, the Cini Foundation, the Marshall Fund, the Club of Rome and certainly not the Tavistock Institute, the Black Nobility of Venice and Genoa. The following is a list of Tavistock brainwashing institutions in the United States, which were noted in my monographs published in 1969:

> ➤ Stanford Research Center. Employs 4,300 people and has an annual budget in excess of $200 million.

> ➤ MIT/Sloane. Employs 5000 people and has an annual budget of $20 million.

> ➤ University of Pennsylvania Wharton School. Employs between 700- 800 people with an annual budget in excess of $35 million.

> ➤ Management and Behavioral Research. Employs 40 people with an annual budget of $2 million.

> ➤ Rand Corporation. Employs in excess of 2000 people with an annual budget of $100 million.

> ➤ National Training Laboratories. Employs 700 people with an annual budget of $30 million.

> ➤ The Hudson Institute. Employs between 120-140 people and has an estimated annual budget of $8 million.

> ➤ Esalen Institute. Employs between 1800-2000 people with an annual budget of in excess of $500 million.

(All 1969 figures)

Thus, in the United States alone, by 1989 we already had a Tavistock Network of between 10 and 20 major institutions, plus 400-500 medium institutions with in excess of 5000 satellites interlocking groups all revolving around Tavistock. Together they employ in excess of 60,000 people, specialists in one way or another in the field of behavioral sciences, mind control, brainwashing, polling and creating public opinion.

And all of them were working against the United States, our Constitution and the Bill of Rights.

Since 1969 these institutions have been expanded and a great many new ones added to the network and are funded not only by large private and corporate donations, but also by the United States Government itself. Tavistock's clients include:

- ➢ The State Department
- ➢ The U.S. Postal Service
- ➢ Department of Defense
- ➢ The CIA: The U.S. Navy Department of Naval Intelligence
- ➢ The National Reconnaissance Office
- ➢ The National Security Council
- ➢ The FBI
- ➢ Kissinger Associates
- ➢ Duke University
- ➢ The State of California
- ➢ Georgetown University and many more.

In the private and corporate areas of our society, Tavistock clients include:

- ➢ Hewlett Packard
- ➢ RCA
- ➢ Crown Zeilerbach
- ➢ McDonald Douglas
- ➢ IBM, Microsoft, Apple Computers, Boeing
- ➢ Kaiser Industries
- ➢ TRW
- ➢ Blythe Eastman Dillon
- ➢ Wells Fargo Bank of America

- Bechtel Corp
- Halliburton
- Raytheon
- McDonnell Douglas
- Shell Oil
- British Petroleum
- Conoco
- Exxon Mobil
- IBM and AT&T.

This is by no means a complete list, which Tavistock guards jealously. These names are just those names I was able to secure. I would say that the majority of Americans are completely unaware that they are in a total war that has been waged against them since 1946; a war of devastating proportions and unremitting pressures; a war we are fast losing, and one which will overwhelm us unless the American people can be shaken loose from their preconceived "it can't happen in America" position.

CHAPTER 32

Exposing the upper level parallel Secret Government

The only way in which we are going to defeat this powerful and insidious enemy is by educating our people, especially our young people in the Constitution, and by standing fast on our Christian faith. Otherwise, our priceless heritage will be lost, forever. The power that Tavistock wields over this nation must be broken.

Hopefully, this work will become a training manual in the hands of millions of Americans, who want to engage the enemy, but who have, hitherto, not been able to identify that enemy.

The political forces controlled by secret societies, all opposing America's republican, constitutional ideals, do not like anything that seeks to expose Tavistock Institute and their disloyalty to America, and even less still, where such disclosures cannot be ridiculed and ignored. Of course those who engage in unmasking the deeds of our secret government invariably pay a high price for such disclosures.

No one who is interested in the future of America can afford to ignore the manner in which Tavistock Institute has whipsawed the American people and manipulated government, even as the majority of Americans remain in ignorance of what is transpiring. With the almost complete control exercised over our nation by our upper-level, parallel, secret government, America has ceased to be a free and independent nation. One can generally fix the beginning of our decline around the time that Woodrow Wilson was "elected" by the British aristocracy.

Most of Tavistock's more recent activities in the United States have centered around the White House and in directing former President G.H.W. Bush, former President Clinton, and President G. W. Bush to engage in war against Iraq. Tavistock is leading the drive to destroy the Second Amendment right of citizens to keep and bear arms.

It has also been instrumental in advising key members of the legislature that they have no further need for the U.S. Constitution, hence the mass of new laws enacted that are not laws at all, since they do not meet the test of constitutionality and fall to the ground.

Tavistock remains the mother of all research facilities in America and Britain, and the leader in behavior modification techniques, mind control and opinion making and shaping.

The Rand Institute at Santa Monica under the direction of Tavistock created the phenomena known as "El Nino" as a weather modification experiment. Tavistock is also heavily engaged in the New Age "UFO" experiments and sighting of aliens, under its mind control contracts with the C.I.A.

Rand Institute runs the ICBM program and does primary analyses for foreign governments. Rand and Tavistock successfully profiled the white population of South Africa as a preliminary to testing the waters for a Communist African National Congress takeover, assisted and strongly supported by the U.S. State Department. "Bishop" Desmond Tutu, who played a leading role in the preamble to the fall of the white government, is a creation of Tavistock.

Georgetown University was taken over in its entirety by Tavistock, back in 1938. Its structure and programs were reformatted to suit the Tavistock "brain trust" blueprint as a center for higher learning. This has had great significance for the United States when we consider that Georgetown University was where Mr. Clinton learned his art of mass manipulation and dissembling.

All State Department field agents are trained at Georgetown. Three of its best-known graduates were Henry Kissinger, William Jefferson Clinton and Richard Armitage. Georgetown's "invisible army" loyalists have done untold harm to the United States and will no doubt play their roles to the full until the end, a time when they will be uprooted, exposed and rendered harmless.

Some of the ugliest and most horrifying actions taken against America were planned at Tavistock. I am referring to the bombing of the Marine compound at Beirut Airport, which took the lives of 200 of our finest young servicemen. One person believed to have been aware of the impending attack by Lebanese terrorists, was Secretary of State George Schultz. As unconfirmed reports stated at the time, Schultz was tipped off in advance of the attack by the Mossad, Israel's secret service agency.

If Schultz did receive such a timely warning, he never relayed it to the Marine base commander at Beirut. Schultz was, and still is, a loyal servant of the Committee of 300 through the Bechtel Corporation.

However, one year after I expressed my suspicions about Schultz and Bechtel (1989), a disaffected high-ranking Mossad agent broke ranks and wrote a book on his experiences.

Parts of the book included the very same information I had printed a year earlier, which has led me to believe that the suspicions I voiced about Schultz in 1989, were not altogether without substance. The whole episode reminds me of the treachery of Gen. Marshall, who deliberately kept information about a pending Japanese air attack against Pearl Harbor from the commander at Hawaii.

There is mounting evidence about an increase in the input and influence Tavistock is having at the CIA. There are great many other intelligence agencies receiving instructions from Tavistock, notably the National Reconnaissance Office (NRO), the Defense Intelligence Agency (DJA), the Treasury Intelligence, and State Department Intelligence.

Every year when the anniversary of the murder of President John Kennedy comes around I am reminded of the leading role played in the planning of his public execution; particularly the part played by MI6. After a 20-year in-depth investigation into the murder of JFK, I think I have come very close to the truth, as detailed in the monograph "The Assassination of President John F. Kennedy. "

The unsolved murder of Pres. Kennedy remains a gross insult against everything the United States stands for. How is it that we, a supposedly free and sovereign nation, allow the cover up of a crime to remain in place, year after year? Surely our intelligence agencies know who the perpetrators of the crime are? Surely we know that the murder of Kennedy was carried out in broad daylight in front of millions of Americans, as an insult, and a warning that the reach of the Committee of 300 goes far beyond what even our highest elected official was able to defend himself against?

The perpetrators of the crime laugh at our confusion secure in the knowledge that they will never be brought to justice, and glorifying in the success of the foul deed and the inability of We, the People, to pierce the corporate veil that hides their faces from view.

The massive cover-up of the Kennedy assassination remains in place. We have full details of how the House Assassinations Committee failed to do its duty, ignoring strong evidence and latching onto flimsy here-say; ignoring the plain fact that the X-rays of Kennedy's head, taken at Bethesda Hospital, were tampered with.

The list of the sins of the Committee of 300 and its servant, the Tavistock Institute is endless. Why did the Senate committee make no effort to investigate the strange disappearance of Kennedy's death certificate; a vital piece of evidence, which should have been found, no matter how long it took and no matter what the cost? Nor was Admiral Burkely, the naval officer who signed the certificate, seriously questioned about the circumstances surrounding the strange—very strange— unexplained disappearance of this vital piece of evidence.

Here I must leave the subject of the murder of John F. Kennedy (which in my opinion was a Tavistock -related project) carried out by MI6 and the FBI Five Division head, Major Louis Mortimer Bloomfield. The CIA is a client of Tavistock's along with literally scores of other U.S. Government agencies. In the decades that have passed since the murder, not one single one of these agencies has ceased to do business with Tavistock. In fact, - Tavistock has added many new names of government agencies to its client list.

In looking through my documents, I discovered that in 1921 when Reese founded Tavistock, he was under the control of British intelligence SIS.

Thus from its inception, Tavistock has always been closely associated with intelligence work, even as it is to this very day. The case of Rudolph Hess may be of more than passing interest to not a few of our readers. It will be recalled that Hess was murdered by two SIS operatives in his Spandau prison cell, the night before he was to be released.

The RIIA was afraid that Hess would blow the lid off what had been kept a dark secret; the close relationship between members of the British oligarchy—including Winston Churchill—and the German Thule Society, of which Hess had been the leader.

Of more than a passing interest is the fact, that the Tavistock Institute was named after the 11th Duke of Bedford, the Marquise of Tavistock. The title was passed on to his son, the 12th Marquise of Bedford. It was to his estate that Hess flew in an attempt to end the war. But Churchill would have none of it and ordered Hess to be arrested and imprisoned. The Duke of Bedford's wife committed suicide by taking an overdose of sleeping pills, when it became apparent that Hess would never be released, even when the war ended.

In my work "Who Murdered Rudolph Hess" and "King Makers, King Breakers—The Cecils", I reveal just how close was this virtual kinship with Hess and other important members of Hitler's inner-circle right up to the start of WWII. Had Hess succeeded in his mission to the Duke of Bedford, Churchill and almost the entire British oligarchy would have been revealed as frauds.

The same thing would have happened had Hess not been kept a solitary prisoner at Spandau in Berlin, guarded for years after the end of WWII by troops drawn from Britain, the United States and the USSR, against all logic and at a tremendous cost (estimated at $50,000 a day).

Because a changed Russia felt they could embarrass America and Britain—especially Britain, they suddenly announced Hess would be released. The British could not afford to run the risk of having their wartime leaders exposed, so the order was given to kill Hess.

Tavistock provides services of a sinister nature to those people we find all across the United States, in every city of note. They have the leading personalities of those cities in the palm of their hand, whether it is in the police department, city government or any other authority.

This is the case in every city also, where the Illuminati and

Freemasons join with Tavistock in exercising their secret powers to walk all over the Constitution and the Bill of Rights.

One can only wonder just how many innocent people are in prison today because they were not knowledgeable about their Constitution and the Bill of Rights; victims of Tavistock, one and all. Pay close attention to the television series, "COPS."

It is standard Tavistock mind control and opinion making fare. In it you find every possible violation of the constitutional rights of persons stopped, and or arrested by the police. It is my firm opinion and belief that "COPS" is meant to condition the public and make us believe that such gross violations of rights we witness is the norm; that the police actually have such excessive powers, and that constitutional safeguards to which every citizen is entitled, do not exist in practice. "COPS" is a most insidious brainwashing, opinion-making controlling program, and it would not be at all surprising to find Tavistock mixed up in it, somewhere.

CHAPTER 33

Interpol in the U.S.:
Its origin and purpose exposed

Among the many international agencies Tavistock serves, is David Rockefeller's private intelligence service, better known as INTERPOL. It is in total dereliction of its legal duty that this illegal entity is allowed to go on functioning on Federal property in Washington, D.C. and under government protection. (U.S. law forbids private foreign police agencies from operating in America. INTERPOL is a private foreign police agency operating on U.S. soil while Congress looks the other way, fearful that one day they might be forced to grasp this noxious nettle, and pull it up by the roots.)

What is INTERPOL? The U.S. Justice Department tries to explain INTERPOL by sidestepping crucial issues. According to its 1988 manual, "Interpol conducts intergovernmental activities, but is not based on an international treaty, convention, or similar legal documents. It was founded upon a constitution drawn up and written by a group of police officers who did not submit it for diplomatic signatures, nor have they ever submitted it for ratification by governments."

How interesting! What an admission! If Interpol does not trample the U.S. Constitution, then nothing does. Where are watchdogs of the House and Senate? Is it that they are afraid of Tavistock and its powerful backer, David Rockefeller? Is the Congress afraid of the Committee of 300?" It certainly seems that way. Interpol is an illegal entity operating within the borders of the United States, without the sanction and approval of We, the

People in flagrant violation of the Constitution of the United States and the constitutions of the 50 States.

Its membership consist of individuals appointed by various national governments without any consultation with the government of the United States. The list of members has never been submitted to a House or Senate committee.

It's presence in the U.S has never been sanctioned by a treaty. This has given rise to series accusations that certain governments under the control of the drug trade: Colombia, Mexico, Panama, Lebanon and Nicaragua, perhaps choose as their representatives, persons involved with the drug trade.

According to Beverly Sweatman of the U.S. Department of Justice National Central Bureau (NCB), (whose existence is itself a violation of the Constitution), this U.S. Government agency exists solely to exchange information with Interpol.

Owned and controlled by David Rockefeller, Interpol is a private agency with a communications network stretching around the globe, heavily involved in one way or another with the drug trade from Afghanistan to Pakistan to the United States.

The interaction of Lt. Colonel Nivaldo Madrin of Panama, Gen. Guillermo Medina Sanchez of Colombia, and certain elements of Mexico's Federal police with Interpol status, point in this direction. Their histories of involvement with the drug trade while serving Interpol are too long to include here, but suffice to say that history is a sordid one.

Yet, in spite of the fact that Interpol is a private organization, it was granted "observer status" by the United Nations (U.N.) in 1975, which stature (totally in violation of the U.N. Charter) enables Interpol to sit at meetings and vote on resolutions, even though it is not a member-country and has no government status. According to the U.N. Charter, only States (in the full definition of the word) can be members of the U.N. Since Interpol is not a state, why does the U.N. violate its Charter?

It is believed that the U.N. is counting heavily on Interpol networks to help it find private arms in the hands of American citizens held by them under their Second Amendment rights, once the U.N. signs a "treaty" with the U.S. Government to disarm all civilian populations of member-states.

Where are America's lawmakers who are supposed to uphold and defend the U.S. Constitution? Where are the great statesmen of yesteryear? Interpol demonstrates, that what we have in their place are politicians turned lawmakers who do not enforce the laws they make, terrified to correct the obvious mistakes that abound on every hand, because, if the were to uphold their oath of office, they would more than likely find themselves without their cushy cozy job.

To recap on some of the information already provided: Tavistock Institute was established in Sussex, England, in 1921 by command of the British monarchy, for the purposes of mind control and public opinion making, and to establish on a carefully-examined scientific basis, at what point the human mind would break down under subjection to prolonged bouts of psychological distress. Elsewhere we shall show that it was first founded in pre-WWI times by the 11th Duke of Bedford, the Marquise of Tavistock.

In the early 1930s, the Rockefeller Brothers Foundation Fund also contributed heavily to Tavistock.

The fact that so many of the chief practitioners of mind control and behavioral modifications were, and are, closely associated with the secret societies that embrace cults of many different ideas and beliefs, notably Isis-Orsiris, Kabala, Sufi, Cathari, Bogomil and Bahai (Manichean) mysticism should be noted.

For the uninitiated, the very idea that prestigious institutions, and their scientists would be involved in cults and even with Satanism and Illuminists would be a very difficult thing to believe. But the connection is very real. We can see just why Tavistock was so interested in these subjects.

Random school shootings by young people subjected to prolonged bouts of stress, and under the influence of habit-forming drugs, are remarkable in that in a large number of these tragic happenings, the perpetrators nearly always claim that they were directed "by voices" to do their deadly work. There can be no doubt that mind control was very much at work in these tragic instances. Unfortunately, we shall see many more such tragic episodes before the public realizes what is going on.

Cultism, mind control, psychological stress application and behavioral modifications are very much a part of what is taught by Tavistock's scientists. In fact, alarmed by leaks showing its connection with Tavistock scientists, the British House of Commons passed a law making it legal for places like Tavistock to conduct what the bill called, "physical research."

Now, the term, "physical research" is so ambiguous as to give rise to serious doubts about what it truly means, or whether, as some critics contended, is merely a term used to cover what really goes on.

In any event, Tavistock was not about to take the public into its confidence. But I can say with absolute certainty that British intelligence MI6 and CIA operatives receive training at Tavistock in metaphysics, mind control, behavior modifications, ESP, hypnotism, the occult, Satanism and Illuminists and the Manichean cults.

These are not just beliefs based on relics from the Middle- Ages. This is evil force being taught in a way that will make a difference to the level of mind control, such as would not have been thought possible a few short years ago. I will make this prediction without fear of contradiction: In later years we are going to discover that all of the random shootings at schools, post offices, shopping malls, were not random shootings at all. They were carried out by conditioned, mind- controlled subjects who were carefully sought out and put on dangerous, mood-altering drugs like Prozac, AZT and Ritalin.

The common denominator between several of the random shootings, starting with David Berkowitz, the so-called "Son of Sam" murderer; all without exception, told investigators that they "heard voices" telling them to shoot people.

The case of Klip Kinkel, the Oregon youth who shot his mother and father, before shooting up his high school is his confession to investigators who interviewed him. Asked why he shot his father and his mother, Kinkel replied that he heard "voices" telling him to shoot them. Nobody will ever be able to prove that Kinkel and the others were victims of mind control experiments carried out by the CIA or that they did indeed "hear voices" induced by through transference carried out by DARPA computer programmers.

The responsible House Oversight Committee must call for the CIA's documents covering mind control and search them for a connection with the school shootings. I believe it is imperative that such an order be sent out to the CIA without any further loss of time.

Apart from my own research into the subject of "physical research," Victor Marachetti, who was with the CIA for 14 years, revealed the existence of a Tavistock-designed physical research program, where CIA operatives tried to contact the spirits of former agents who had died. As I said in my above mentioned monograph, I have had a great deal of personal experience in the "metaphysical" realms and know for a fact, that a large number of British and American intelligence agents are indoctrinated in it.

Tavistock calls it "behavioral science," and it has advanced so rapidly in the last ten years that it has become one of the most important types of training agents can undergo. In Tavistock's ESP programs, each participant is a "volunteer", who agrees to have his personality "correlated" with ESP; that is to say, they have agreed to help Tavistock find an answer as to why certain people are psychic and others are gifted with ESP.

The object of the exercise is to make each and every MI6 and CIA agent highly psychic with sharply developed ESP. Because a number of years have passed since I was directly involved in such matters, I consulted a colleague who is still in the "service", to find out how successful Tavistock has been with its experiments? He told me that Tavistock has indeed perfected its techniques and that it was now possible to make selected MI6 and CIA operatives "ESP-Perfect." Here it is necessary to explain that the CIA and MI6 maintain a very high degree of secrecy about such matters.

The majority of intelligence agents who are in the programs are for the most part members of the Illuminati and or Freemasonry, or both. In short, the "long range penetration" technique applied with such success to the normal world is now being applied to the spirit world!

Tavistock's "Long Range Penetration and Inner Directional Conditioning", developed by Dr. Kurt Lewin, whom we have already met a few times, is primarily a program where thought control is practiced on mass groups. What gave rise to the program was the British Army Psychological Warfare Bureau's all-pervasive use of propaganda in WWI. The extensive propaganda it ran was intended to convince the British workingman that war was necessary. Another part of it was to convince the British public that Germany was an enemy, and its leader a veritable demon.

This massive effort had to be launched between 1912 and 1914 because the British working class did not believe that Germany wanted war, anymore than the British people wanted it, and did not even dislike the Germans. All that public perception had to be changed. A secondary, though no less important task for the bureau was to get America into the war. A key element in that plan was to provoke Germany into sinking the "Lusitania" a large trans-Atlantic liner built along the lines of the doomed Titanic.

In spite of warnings in press advertisements in a New York newspaper that the ship had been converted into an Armed Merchant Cruiser (AMC) and was therefore fair game in accordance with the Geneva Conventions, the Lusitania sailed for Liverpool carrying a full compliment of passengers, among them many hundreds of American passengers.

The ship's holds were packed with a large compliment of munitions destined for the British Army, forbidden under international the rules of war to be carried by passenger liners.

At the time it was hit by a single torpedo, the Lusitania was essentially an Armed Merchant Cruiser (AMC). The press on both sides of the Atlantic was filled with accounts of German barbarity and unprovoked attack on a defenseless passenger liner, But the American and British public who still needed a lot more "conditioning" did not buy the story. They felt there was "something rotten in the State of Denmark." The sinking of the Lusitania with heavy loss of life was the type of "contrived situation" that President Wilson needed and it inflamed American public opinion against Germany.

Profiting from this experience, the British Army Bureau of Psychological Warfare set up the Tavistock Institute for Human Relations on the orders of the British monarchy and placed British newspaper magnate, Alfred Harmsworth, the son of a barrister born in Chapelizod near Dublin. He was later awarded the title the 12th Duke of Bedford, Lord Northcliffe.

In 1897, as a run-up to the war that was coming, Harmsworth sent one of his writers by the name of G.W. Steevens to Germany for the purpose of writing a serialized sixteen part article entitled Under the Iron Heel.

In true reverse psychology the articles were lavish in their praise of the German Army while in the same breath warning that the British nation would be defeated if war broke out against Germany.

In 1909, Northcliffe commissioned Robert Blatchford, a senior Socialist to go to Germany and write articles about what a danger the German Army posed to Britain. Blatchford's theme was that he believed from his observations that Germany was "deliberately preparing to destroy the British Empire." It was in line with Northcliffe's prediction published in the Daily Mail (one of his newspapers) in 1900 that there would be war between Germany and Britain. Northcliffe wrote an editorial saying that Britain needed to use a greater part of its budget for defense spending.

When the war broke out, Northcliffe was accused by the editor of The Star newspaper of having propagated a climate of war. "Next to the Kaiser, Lord Northcliffe has done more than any living man to bring about the war."

The poor editor did not know that he himself had become a victim of propaganda, as the Kaiser had done little to promote war and was looked upon with some disdain by the British military establishment. Historians are in general agreement that the Kaiser was in no position to control the Germany Army. It was General Ludendorff to who The Star should have referred. It was Northcliffe, who began agitating for conscription from the very day that war broke out between the two nations.

This was to be an institution where every aspect of mass brainwashing and public conditioning would be brought to a fine art. A policy and set of rules were established, culminating in Tavistock's 1930 "Long Range Penetration and Inner Directional Conditioning," that was unleashed against Germany in 1931.

In the period before the first years of WWII, Roosevelt, (himself a 33rd degree Mason and a member of the Illuminati through the Society of Cincinnati,) sought Tavistock's help in getting American into the war. Roosevelt was under the direction of the "300" to help pull British chestnuts out of the fire, but to do so, he needed a major incident to latch on to.

All during the period 1939 - 1941 U.S. Navy submarines based out of Iceland attacked and sank German shipping, although neutrality laws forbad engaging in hostilities with the combatants. But Germany would not be drawn into retaliating. The major incident that was to precipitate America's entry into WWII was Japan's attack on Pearl Harbor. This was a Tavistock conspiracy against both nations. In order to foster such an attack, Secretary of State Marshall refused to meet with Japan's envoys seeking to head off the coming conflict.

Marshall also deliberately delayed warning his commander at Pearl Harbor until after the attack had begun. In short, Roosevelt and Marshall both knew about the pending attack, but deliberately ordered the information to be withheld from their officers on the ground at Pearl Harbor. Tavistock had told Roosevelt that "only a major incident" would get America into WWII. Stimson, Knox and Roosevelt knew about the impending attack, but did nothing to stop it.

From time to time thoughtful people have asked me: "But wouldn't leaders like Lord Haig, Churchill, Roosevelt, and Bush realize how many lives would be lost in a world war?"

The answer is that as programmed individuals, the "great men" didn't care about the high cost of human life. General Haig—a noted Freemason/Illuminist/Satanist— declared on more than one occasion his dislike of the British lower classes, and he proved it by throwing wave after of wave of "common British soldiers" against impregnable German lines, a tactic any decent military strategist would have shunned.

As a result of Haig's callous disregard for his own troops, hundreds of thousands of young British soldiers from the "lower classes" died tragically and needlessly. This made the British public hate Germany, exactly as the British Army Psychological Warfare Bureau had predicted. Much of what I have included in this book I deliberately held back in the first exposure. I did not feel that the American people were ready to understand the metaphysical side of Tavistock. You can't feed a baby on meat; milk comes first. By introducing Tavistock in this way, many minds were opened, which otherwise would have remained closed.

CHAPTER 34

The cults of the East India Company

For centuries the British oligarchy has been the home of occultism, the metaphysical, mysticism and mind control. Bulwer Lytton wrote "The Secrets of the Egyptian Book of the Dead", and so many of Annie Besant's adherents of the Theosophist Society came from British upper classes, which even today is popular with them. The descendants of the Catharists and Albigensians of Southern France and Northern Italy had migrated to England and adopted the name "Savoyard." Before them came the Bogomils of the Balkans and Pelicans of Asia Minor. All these sects had originated from the Babylonian Manicheans.

Inroads were made into this type of occultism by the Tavistock Institute, using some of its mind control techniques developed by Kurt Lewin and his team of researchers. (See "The Committee of 300" for details.)

The East India Company (EIC) and later, the British East India Company (BEIC) was the original "300," whose descendants rule the world today. Opium and the drug trade was the stock in trade then, and remained so. From this highly organized, complex structure, grew Socialism, Marxism, Communism and National Socialism and Fascism.

Beginning in 1914, extensive mind control experiments were carried out at Cold Spring Harbor in New York, the race-eugenics center sponsored by Mrs. E.E, Harriman, mother of Averill Harriman, governor of New York State at the time, who became a prominent public and political figure in the U.S. and Europe.

The grand lady poured millions of dollars of her money into the project and invited German scientists to share the forum. A great many of Tavistock's mind control techniques especially "reverse psychology" technique taught by Reese, originated at Tavistock, which today, forms the basis of mind-controlling exercises to implant the notion in the minds of the American public that the black and colored races are superior to the white race, "racism" in reverse.

German scientists were invited to attend Cold Harbor indoctrinations by Mrs. Harriman and her group, comprised of some of the leading citizens of the period (1915). After a year or two at Cold Spring Harbor, the German contingent returned to Germany, and under Hitler, put race eugenics learned at Cold Spring Harbor, into practice. All this information lay hidden from the American people until it was exposed in my book "Codeword Cardinal" and in my several monographs, which preceded the book and subsequently in my work "Aids-The Full Disclosure."

Tavistock and the White House

Tavistock mind conditioning techniques have been consistently in use in the United States by some of the highest and most important political figures in our history, beginning with Woodrow Wilson and continuing with Pres. Roosevelt. Every U.S. President after Roosevelt has been under the control of the "300" and the Tavistock Institute.

Roosevelt was a typical mind-controlled programmed subject trained in Tavistock methodology. He would talk peace while preparing for war. He seized powers he was not entitled to under the U.S. Constitution, citing the illegal actions of President Wilson as his authority, and then explained away his actions through "fireside chats," which was a Tavistock idea to deceive the American people. Like another Tavistock robot, James Earl Carter, and Pres. Bush, his successor, convinced the American people that everything he did, no matter how blatantly unconstitutional, was done for their benefit. This was unlike Roosevelt, who knew full well when he was doing wrong, but who nevertheless, relished his task and carried out his Tavistock-British royal family mandate with gusto, and with total disregard for human life, as is common to all cultists.

When Pres. Bush, the elder, ordered invasion of Panama, it was a blatantly unconstitutional action at the cost of the lives of 7,000 Panamanians over which Mr. Bush never lost any sleep, nor did he blink an eye over the death of 150.000 Iraqi soldiers in the undeclared (illegal) war against Iraq that was to follow his "trial run" to gauge public opinion.

Carter was no stranger to the occult; one of his sisters was a leading witch in America. Carter believed that he was a "born again Christian," even though his entire political career was shot through with Socialist and Communist ideals and principles, which he never hesitated to put into practice. Carter is a true split personality product of Tavistock. This was noted by Hugh Sidey, a well-known columnist for mainstream media who wrote in July of 1979: "The Jimmy Carter now at work behind the closed doors of the White House is not the Jimmy Carter we grew to know in the first 30 days of his presidency."

Carter, programmed by Tavistock graduate Dr. Peter Bourne, had been through the hands of another Tavistock psychologist, Admiral Hymen Rickover, during Carter's stint at Annapolis.

Carter was pre-selected by the Rothschilds as being admirably suitable for special training, and one who would be "adaptable to changing circumstances", willing to depart from principles.

John Foster Dulles was another Tavistock indoctrinated figure of note that was close to the White House, holding the position of

Secretary of State. Dulles blatantly lied to a U.S. Senate Committee during the United Nations (UN) hearings, brazenly testifying under oath about the constitutionality of the U.S. belonging to this world body.

Dulles dazzled and deceived the senators as to the constitutionality of the U.S. joining the U.N. and swayed enough senators to vote in favor if the so-called treaty, which is not a treaty, but an ambiguous agreement.

The U.S. Constitution does not recognize "agreements", only treaties signed by the nations concerned. However the problem Dulles had was that the U.N. is not a country, so Tavistock got around the impediment by advising the State Department to call the document, an "agreement." Dulles was a Satanist, Illuminist, and a member of a number of occult societies.

George Herbert Walker Bush is another "product trained" certified graduate of Tavistock's mind control system. The actions of this 33rd Degree Mason, in Panama and Iraq, speak volumes.

In Panama, acting under the orders of the RIIA and the CFR, Bush, the elder, moved to protect drug money in the Rockefeller owned banks in Panama, after General Noriega had exposed two of them as money laundering facilities in the drug trade chain.

Bush ordered U.S. Armed forces to invade Panama without having the authority expressed in the only constitutional way, a joint declaration of war by the U.S. House and Senate of the Congress, and in gross violation of his constitutional powers as President.

The office of the president is expressly forbidden war-making powers by the Founding Fathers. But notwithstanding the lack of empowerment, Bush repeated his gross violations of the U.S. Constitution in ordering the U.S. Armed forces to invade Iraq, again without a the mandated declaration of war and in excess of his powers. The "inner conditioned" American public, the shell-shocked victims of Tavistock's war on them, did not turn a hair as they watched the Constitution being ripped to shreds.

Her Majesty Queen Elizabeth II, warmly praised Bush, the elder, for his "successful" war against Iraq, and knighted him for his acts of defiance of the U.S. Constitution. This is not the first time that Elizabeth had rewarded American law breakers with high honors.

British and American cultists and Illuminists in the oil cartels are still carrying out a war of attrition against Iraq in 2005. They will not stop until they have laid their greedy, bloodstained hands on Iraq's oil riches in the manner in which Milner stole the gold from the Boers in the Anglo- Boer War (1899-1903.)

Do you find yourself responding to this information in a "maladaptive way"? Do you say, "These actions cannot be the actions of an American President? This is nonsense.

If this is your maladaptive response, then turn your attention to the Boer War and you will soon see that Bush was only emulating the Satanic barbarity of General Lord Kitchener and Lord Milner in their war of extermination against the Boer nation. Also, it behooves us to recall that the tragedy of Waco began on the Bush watch, and that vendetta against David Koresh was carried on by the leader of the Republican Party.

While Attorney General Reno and Clinton carried out the actual policy of destruction for which Koresh was slated, George Bush played a leading role in the ghastly tableaux in which Koresh and 87 of his followers died.

Although it is not generally known, Tavistock had a hand in the planning and might even have directed the onslaught by the FBI and the ATF on Koresh and the Davidians. Tavistock was represented by units of the British SAS who had been involved in training the ATF and the FBI on how to destroy Koresh and his followers and burn their church to the ground. Waco was unholy black arts Satanism in action, no more and no less.

The fiery end of Koresh and his followers was typical Satanism at work, even though most of those who participated in the high crime and violations of human rights and the violation of the 1st, 2nd, 5th and 10th Amendment rights of the victims, were not aware that they were in the hands of Satanists. They did not have the faintest inkling that they were being used by spiritual forces of the darkest kind.

Tavistock's massive brainwashing of the America turned the public against Koresh and the Davidians, setting the stage for the destruction of lives and property at Waco, in utter defiance of the Constitution and the Bill of Rights.

The wanton destruction of innocent lives and property by agents of the Federal Government who had no jurisdiction in the State of Texas (or any other State for that matter) and consequently, no authority to do what they did—violated the 10th Amendment, the citizen' protection against excesses by the Federal Government. The State of Texas did not step in and stop the violation of the 10th Amendment that was in progress at Waco as it was the Governor's duty to do under the U.S. Constitution and the Constitution of the State of Texas.

Tavistock had come a long way since Ramsey McDonald was sent to the United States in 1895 to "spy out the land for Socialism." Ramsey reported back to the Fabians that for the U.S. to become a Socialist state, the State and Federal constitutions (in that order) had to be destroyed; Waco was the embodiment of that goal.

John Marshall, the Third Chief Justice of the United States, and the Lopez case decided by the 9th Circuit Court of Appeals, for once and for all made it clear that Federal Agents had no jurisdiction inside the borders of the States except where counterfeiting of U.S. dollars was being investigated. This in itself is an oxymoron, as so-called "U.S. dollars" are not U.S. dollars, but "Federal Reserve Notes"- not the currency of the United States—but the notes of a privately-owned non-governmental central bank.

Why protect fraud, even if it is being perpetrated by the U.S. Government? When the Constitution was written, the Founding Fathers felt that their denial of a central bank would prevent any bogus operation like the Federal Reserve coming into being. The constitutional provision protects U.S. Treasury Notes from being counterfeited. It is doubtful whether a Federal Reserve note, which is not a U.S. dollar, enjoys the protection of the U.S. Constitution.

At Waco, the Sheriff failed in his duty to order Tavistock's agents and the FBI out of the county, as the FBI was not investigating counterfeiting in conformity with the U.S. Constitution. The FBI was at Waco illegally. It was all a part of a carefully planned exercise to ascertain just how far the Federal Government could go in violating the Constitution before being brought up short.

Just as the British lower and middle classes were inflamed against Germany at the commencement of WWI, through propaganda lies that the Kaiser had ordered his soldiers to cut off the arms of little children when they invaded Belgium and Holland, just so Tavistock programmed Americans to hate Koresh.

Tavistock's blast of lies about Koresh went out over the airwaves, day and night: Koresh was having sex with very young children in the "compound." His church, a simple wooden structure, was labeled a "compound" by the mind controllers at Tavistock. Another of Tavistock's gross lies was that the Davidians were running an amphetamine lab in the "compound".

"Compound" became the Tavistock-coined buzzword.

That Clinton gave the go-ahead to have the Davidians, gassed, shot at, subjected to devilish music night and day, and finally, burnt alive, is not surprising. Through the late Pamela Harriman Mr. Clinton was introduced to Tavistock and passed its mind control indoctrination initiation, during his stay at Oxford. Thereafter, he was introduced to Socialism/Marxism/Communism before being approved by Tavistock to succeed Mr. Bush, the elder, who had outlived his usefulness.

Tavistock planned and executed a massive media drive using their polling profiling to implant Clinton in the minds of the American people, as one well suited to run the nation.

It was Tavistock that arranged the strictly controlled Clinton interview with CBS, after Geniffer Flowers revealed that he had been her lover for the past 12 years, and it was Tavistock that took control of the reaction of the American people in the aftermath of the CBS interview. Thus, through its far-flung network of polling and opinion-making assets the Clinton presidency was not torpedoed, although without Tavistock having been in control from start to finish of the CBS interview, it is certain that Clinton would have been forced to resign in disgrace.

If you are looking for proof; if your response is "maladaptive", then compare Clinton's escape with Gary Hart's conviction on a far lesser charge. The first "New Age of Aquarius" White House lawyer to be trained in Tavistock methodology was Mark Fabiani. His deft handling of situations, which every single observer expected would sink Clinton, became the talk of Washington.

Only 13 people in the inner circle of the Illuminati and the Freemason hierarchy knew what the secret of Fabiani's success was Lanny Davis, who took over from Fabiani, enjoyed even greater success. Known as "Dr. Spin", Davis outflanked and outfoxed two special prosecutors, Judge Walsh and Kenneth Starr blunted every attack launched by the Republicans in Congress, leaving the Republican Party in total disarray.

This Tavistock-trained lawyer carried out an audacious raid against Clinton's host of enemies in Congress. Davis' masterstroke came with the Thompson Committee hearings into DNC campaign funding and a host of Arkansas scandals.

The Tavistock plan was simple, and like all simple plans, it was a stroke of genius. Davis collected every newspaper in the country, which had ever carried even the smallest story about Clinton's misdeeds, fund raising scandals and Whitewater. On the very day the Thompson committee was in full cry, baying for the blood of the President, one of the many assistants serving Davis threaded his way through the packed hearing room, and gave each of the committee members a file of clippings compiled by Davis.

With the file came a memo signed by Davis: What the committee was investigating at the cost of millions of dollars was nothing but a collection of "old news". What was there to investigate when the charges against Clinton were yesterday's news?

The Thompson Committee had been bushwhacked and thereafter ran out of steam and went out of action, a great victory for Tavistock and the White House. Prime Minister Blair was to use the same formula in disarming Parliamentary critic's charges that he had lied about his reasons for going to war alongside Bush the younger. The "Daily Mirror" accounts were all "old news," Blair said in responding to what might have been a damning question. The MP asking the question was leading a move to have Blair impeached. Instead of answering, Blair deflected the question. Under Parliamentary rules, the MP had had his "turn" and would not get another opportunity to try and force the truth out of Blair.

CHAPTER 35

The music industry, mind control, propaganda and war

We should note that Tavistock's influence in America has expanded since it began its own bureaus here in 1946. Tavistock has brought the art of disinformation to a fine- tuned pitch. Such disinformation campaigns start with carefully crafted rumors. These are, generally speaking, planted in right wing circles, where they grow and spread like wildfire. Tavistock has long known that the right wing is a fertile breeding ground for rumors to grow and be spread.

In my experience, hardly a day passes that I am not asked to confirm some rumor or another, usually by people who should know better. The clever strategy of spreading disinformation through rumor has a double benefit:

1) It gives a semblance of credence to stories planted on conservatives.
2) By the time the information is proved to be false, the disinformation has tainted its purveyors to the extent where they may safely be described as "crackpots", "the paranoid fringe of the conservatives", "extremists" and a whole lot worse.

The next time you hear one of these kinds of rumors, think long and hard about the source of the rumor before you pass it along. Remember how Tavistock manipulators work: The juicier the rumor, the greater is your inclination to spread it, will unwittingly make you a part of Tavistock's insidious disinformation machine.

Turning now to another area of expertise in which Tavistock initiates its graduates, we refer to the assassination of politicians of importance who cannot be bought, and who have to be silenced. The murders of U.S. Presidents Lincoln, Garfield, McKinley, and Kennedy are all linked to British intelligence MI6, and since 1923, associated with the Tavistock Institute.

Pres. Kennedy proved to be impervious to mind control by Tavistock, so was chosen for public execution as a warning to those who would aspire to power, that none was higher than the Committee of 300.

The grisly spectacle of the public execution of Kennedy was a message to the American people; one which they may not, even now, be aware of. Perhaps the Tavistock Institute provided the blueprint for Kennedy's execution. Perhaps it also carefully selected each and every participant, starting with the obviously mind-controlled Lee Harvey Oswald, and to the not so obvious Lyndon Johnson. Those who would not comply, or who sought to bring out the truth, suffered a variety of punishment, from disgrace, hounding from public life, and even death.

We leave Tavistock's control of U.S. Presidents, past, and future, and turn our attention to the music and entertainment industry. Nowhere is mind control "brainwashing" of huge segments of the American public so noticeable, as it is in "the music and entertainment industry. Decades later, misguided, uninitiated people still get angry with me over my exposure of the "Beatles" as a Tavistock project. Now, I fully expect the same people who tell me that they know all about the history of the "Beatles"; that they are musicians and I am not, to question the following:

Did you know that so-called "Rap" music is another Tavistock program? So is "Hip-Hop." As inane and idiotic as the words are (one can hardly call them "lyrics,") these words have been crafted by the technician in mind control and behavior modification, so that they would fit in and became an integral part of Tavistock's gang wars program for America's major cities. The chief purveyors of this "music" and indeed all so-called "Rock" and "Pop" music (excuse the use of Tavistock jargon) are:

- ➤ Time Warner.
- ➤ Sony.
- ➤ Bertelsman.
- ➤ EMI.
- ➤ The Capital Group.
- ➤ Seagram Canada
- ➤ Philips Electronic.
- ➤ The Indies.

Time Warner

Annual revenues $23.7 billion (1996 figures). Its music publishing business owns one million songs through its subsidiary, Warner, Chappell. These include songs by Madonna, and Michael Jackson. It prints and publishes sheet music. Time Warner "Rap" and "Pop" labels include Amphetamine Reptile, Asylum Sire, Rhino, Maverick, Revolution, Luka Bop, Big Head Todd and The Monsters marketed through Warner REM.

Time Warner also distributes alternative music labels through its subsidiary. Alternative Distribution Alliance, which covers the greater part of Europe, and which is particularly strong in England and Germany. It is not by accident that these two countries have been targeted by the manipulators at Tavistock.

The mostly subliminal, but increasingly open incitement to violence, unrestrained sex, anarchism and Satanism, is found in abundance among the songs owned by Time Warner. This almost cult-like dominance of the youth of Western Europe (and since the fall of the USSR, it is creeping into Russia and Japan also) is menacing civilization in Europe that has taken thousands of years to build up and mature. The huge following of youth and its seemingly insatiable appetite for this kind of utter junk "music" is frightening to behold, as is Tavistock's grip on the minds of those who listen to it.

Time Warner distributes music through music clubs, which it owns outright, or else is in partnership with others. Columbia House is one example. Sony has a 50% share in Columbia House.

Time Warner's manufacturing division, WEA, makes CDs; CD-ROMS, Audios, Videos, digital versatile discs, while another subsidiary, Ivy Hill, prints CD covers and inserts. American Family Enterprises, another subsidiary, markets music, books and magazines in a 50% holding with Heartland Music.

Time Warner Motion Pictures has studios and production companies comprising, Warner Bros; Castle Rock Entertainments; New Line Cinemas. Time Warner Motion Pictures owns 467 screens in the U.S. and 464 screens in Europe. (1989 figures: The numbers are much greater today in 2005.)

Its broadcasting network includes WB Network, Prime Star; Cinemax, Comedy; Central Court TV; SEGA Channel; Turner Classic Movies (Ted Turner owns 10% of the stock in Time Warner).

It broadcasts to China, Japan, New Zealand, France and Hungary. Its Cable Franchise lists 12.3 million subscribers.

TV/Production/Distribution includes Warner Bros Television; HBO Independent Productions, Warner Bros. Television Animations; Telepictures Productions; Castle Rock Television; New Line Television, Citadel Entertainment; Hanna Barbara Cartoons; World Championship Wrestling; Turner Original

Productions; Time Warner Sports; Turner Learning; Warner Home Videos and in its library it has 28,500 television titles and animated shorts.

Time Warner owns CNN Radio, which acquired from Ted Turner. It also owns 161 retail outlet stores, Warner Books, Littel, Brown, Sunset Books, Oxmoor House and the Book of the Month Club.

Time Warner owns the following magazines: People; Sports Illustrated; Time; Fortune; Life; Money; Entertainment; Weekly; Progressive Farmer; Southern Accents; Parenting; Health; Hippocrates; Asiaweek; Weight Watchers; Mad Magazine; D.C. Comics; American Express Travel and Leisure; Food and Wine. Time Warner also owns a number of Theme Parks: Six Flags; Warner Bros; Movie World; Sea World of Australia.

I hope that at this point the reader will pause to reflect upon the enormous power for good or evil which rests in the hands of Time Warner. Obviously, this giant could make or break anybody. And then, remember, it is a client of the Tavistock Institute. It is frightening to contemplate what this mighty machine could do to public opinion and shaping the minds of the young, as we have seen with "Gay Days" at Disney World.

SONY

Sony's revenues in 1999 were estimated at $48.7 billion. It is the largest electronics company in the world. Its music division control Rock/Rap/Pop; Columbia; Rutthouse; Legacy Recordings; Sony Independent Label; MIJ Label; (Michael Jackson); Sony Music Nashville; Columbia Nashville. Sony owns thousands of Rock/Pop labels including Bruce Springsteen; So-So Def; Slam Jazz; Bone Thugs in Harmony; Rage Against the Machine; Razor Sharp; Ghost-Face Killa; Crave; and Ruthless Relativity.

If you have ever stopped to wonder how this awful idiocy with its highly suggestive word and incitement to violence got so big in such a short time, now you know. It is backed to the hilt by Sony. Tavistock has long regarded Rap as a useful messenger to precede anarchy and chaos—which is getting closer and closer.

Sony distributes Punk Alternative rock label Epitaph Record; Hell Cat; Rancid; Crank Possum Records and Epitome Surf Music by Blue Sting Ray. In addition Sony publishes music through Sony/ATV Music Publishing. Sony owns all of Michael Jackson's "songs" and nearly the entire range of the "Beatles."

Sony owns Loews Theatres, Sony Theatres, and its television interests include network game shows. It has about 15% of the market in music sales, sheet music, and is the largest international music company in the world. Sony's other products are CD records, optical discs, audio and videotapes.

Loews Hotel property in Monte Carlo is a clearinghouse of information for drug trafficking, and its employees report directly to the Monet Carlo police, any "suspicious activity" going on in the hotel.

("Suspicious" mean any outsiders trying to bust into the trade.) Several of the senior level front desk employees are Monte Carlo police-trained to keep and eye on things.

This is not to stamp out drug dealing; it is merely to keep "upstarts" getting into the drug trade. "Outsiders" arriving in Loews Hotel are informed on and are promptly arrested. Such events are sold to the press and world news media as "drug busts." Sony's Motion Pictures Division consists of Columbia Pictures; Tri-Star Pictures; Sony Pictures; Classic Triumph; Triumph Films with rights to Columbia Home Tri-Star movies. Its television interests include network game shows.

Bertelsman's A.G.

A German privately held company owned by Reinhard Mohn, its estimated revenues were $15.7 billion in 1999. Bertelsman owns 200 music labels from 40 countries, which labels cover Rap/Rock/Pop. Whitney Houston; The Grateful Dead: Bad Boys: Ng Records, Volcano Enterprises; Dancing Cat; Addict; Gee Street (Jungle Brothers) and Global Soul. All these contain explicit incitement to sex aberrations, drug taking, anarchy, and violence. Bertelsman's owns Country & Western properties Arista Nashville (Pam Tillis); Career (LeRoy Parnell) RCA Label Group; BNA (Lorrie Morgan.) Other titles it owns are the sound track from Star Wars; Boston Pops; New Age and Windham Hill etc. The company publishes sheet music through BMG Music, which controls the rights to 700,000 songs, including The Beach Boys; B.B. King; Barry Manilow; 100,000 Famous Music of Paramount Studios. It own seven music clubs in the U.S. and Canada, and makes credit cards for MBNA Bank.

Bertelsman A.G does tremendous book business worldwide and is very much a Committee of 300 affiliate.

Bertelsmann holdings include Doubleday; Dell Publishers; Family Circle; Parent and Child; Fitness; American Homes and Gardens, with 38 magazines in Spain, France, Italy, Hungary and Poland. Bertelsman's television and satellite channels are in Europe, where it is the largest broadcaster. This company is very vindictive and will not hesitate to attack anyone who dares to reveal what it thinks might not be in the company's best interests.

EMI

A British-based company with estimated revenues of $6 billion in 1999, the company owns sixty music labels in forty-six countries: Rock/Pop/Rap; Beetle Boys; Chrysallis; Grand Royal; Parlaphone; Pumpkin Smashers; Virgin; Point Blank.

EMI owns and controls The Rolling Stones; Duck Down; No Limit; N00 Tribe; Rap-A-Lot (The Ghetto Boys) with an immense sheet music publishing business. It has a direct interest or owns outright 231 stores in seven countries, including HMV; Virgin Megastores: Dillons (USA). EMI has network stations throughout Britain and Europe, some of which work in conjunction with Bertelsmann.

The Capital Group

This Los Angeles-based investment group sold 35% of its stock to Seagram's, the Bronstein's liquor company and a high-ranking Committee of 300 property. Seagram's has an 80% stake in Universal Music Group (formerly MCA) now Matushita Electric Industries property.

Its 1999 revenues were estimated as $14 billion. Seagram owns in excess of 150,000 copyrights, including the copyrights to Impact: Mechanic; Zebra; Radioactive Records; Fort Apache Records; Heavy D and the Boys.

The Capital Group has joint ventures with Steven Spielberg, Jeffrey Katzenburg and David Geffen. In its Country and Western Division, the company owns Reba McIntyre, Wynona, George Straight; Dolly Parton; Lee Anne Rimes and Hank Williams.

Through Seagram, the company owns concert halls at Fiddler's Green (Denver); Blossom Music Center (Cleveland); Gorge Amphitheater (Washington State); Starplex (Dallas). It has expanded to Toronto and Atlanta. The Capital Group through its Motion Pictured Division owns Demi Moore, Danny De Vito, Penny Marshall and a host of minor figures in the movie-making business. Universal Films Library is a Capital Group property, as is Universal Films Library. The company owns 500 retail stores, several hotels as well as Universal Studios in Hollywood.

The Indies

One of the smaller companies in the music and entertainment, its annual revenues is estimated at $5.billion. The company has a substantial portfolio of Rock/Rap/Pop labels, mostly of the more bizarre kind.

Its Country and Western Division owns Willie Nelson and distribution is done through "The Big Six." Even without ownership of any independent retail stores or outlets, the company managed to capture an astonishing 21% of U.S. music sales.

The significance of this is that most of its revenues come from bizarre Rap/Pop/Rock sales of the violent, abusive, foul language, sexually-suggestive titles, anarchy—which shows the way the youth of America is going.

Philips Electronic

This Dutch company had revenues of $15.8 billion in 1996. While it is mainly an electronics company, it is in the "Big Six" category primarily because of ownership of 75% of Polygram Music. Its portfolio of labels is in Rock/Pop/Rap. Elton John is one of its properties. Philips ranks third in the music publishing business with 375,000 copyright titles.

Through its subsidiaries in Europe and Britain, in 1998 Philips produced 540 million CD's and VHS tapes. Its Motion Pictures Division owns Jodi Foster, while Philips Television own Robert Redford's Sundance Films and Propaganda Films.

The foregoing information should give you, the reader, and some idea of the immense power this giant industry wields over our daily lives; how it is shaping the minds of the youth of America. Without the control and the advanced techniques made available to these companies through Tavistock, the giant strides the industry has made would not have been possible. The information I have provided should shake you to your very foundations when you come to the realization that Tavistock controls what "news" we see, what "home movies" and television network movies we are allowed to see; what music we listen to.

Behind this gigantic enterprise stands the Tavistock Institute for Human Relations. As I have clearly demonstrated, America is marching in lock-step with the gigantic movie- music industry; hitherto unknown forces— powerful forces whose sole aim and object is to pervert, twist and distort the minds of our youth, to make it all the easier for the Committee of 300 to usher in the Socialist New World Order - One World Government, in which the new Communists rule of the world.

The information I have put before you should be a source of great alarm as you contemplate the future of your children and the youth of America, having come to the knowledge and understanding that they are being fed a diet of anarchistic ideas, revolutionary fervor, and incitement to take drugs, free sex, abortion, lesbianism and homosexual acceptance.

Without this giant music and entertainment industry, Michael Jackson would only have been the puerile, insipid nonentity, but he was "puffed" and Tavistock told the youth of our land just how great he is, and how much they, - the youth of the Western world love him! It also has to do with the power to control the media.

Inasmuch as the music and entertainment industry is what I call an "open secret" designed by Tavistock, I do not expect my work on this vital subject to be accepted as the whole truth, at least up to the year 2015, which is the year I anticipate the outbreak of "Armageddon" the all-out nuclear- CAB war, when the full wrath of God will fall on the United States of America. But with regard to massive media control it is not difficult for even the untrained observer to see, hear and read that indeed, the U.S. has a controlled media, the product of the Tavistock Institute. This factor is what got President Bush elected, and then, to the astonishment of all of Europe and at least half of the American voters, saw him elected for a second term in spite of his deplorable record.

How did this happen? The question is easily answered: Due to the breakdown of America's national media. Traditional broadcasters abandoned their obligation to promote the public interest; they no longer felt an obligation to report two sides of the questions.

The national media intensified its policy of "mixing news with fiction" that began with "War of Worlds. "

While this attracted viewers and increased revenues it did nothing for the long-held doctrine of fairness in broadcasting so essential to the flow of information in a free society. In recent years this grave problem has been exacerbated by the rise of the rightwing "thunder squad" who will tolerate no contra-opinion but. They broadcast only the Bush administration's opinion, and they are not above twisting and "spinning" the news in the best Tavistock manner.

This was confirmed by a joint survey in 2004 carried out by the Center on Policy Studies, the Center on Policy Attitudes, the Program on International Policy Attitudes, and the Center for International and Security Studies. What they found is really the key to why Bush is still in the White House, and a tribute to the power of professional propaganda:

> 75 percent of the Bush faithful were not convinced by the President Commission's finding that Iraq had nothing to do with Al Qaeda.

> The majority of Bush supporters believed that a greater part of the Islamic world supported the U.S. in its invasion of Iraq. This is totally at variance with the facts. Egypt, a Muslim state does not support the USA and the majority of Egyptians want the U.S. out of Iraq. Turkey, which although a secular state is overwhelmingly

Muslim, by a vote of 87 percent is opposed to the U.S. being in Iraq and reject the reasons given for the invasion.

➤ Seventy percent of the Bush faithful believe that Iraq possessed WMD's.

What I have written here is the indisputable truth, but it will take a major event to confirm it as such, just as it took 14 years for my Committee of 300 book and 25 years for my Club of Rome Report to be confirmed by Alexander King himself. But let there be no doubt that Tavistock, today, in 2005, is in full control of every aspect of life in America. Not one thing escapes its notice.

In 2005 we are witness to the amazing influence and power of the Tavistock Institute and its upper-level masters, the Committee of 300 in the manner in which the United States is run by President George Bush and the acceptance of what Bush says and does without question or doubt.

The reasons for these mistaken beliefs are not hard to find. The Bush administration told the American public many times in 1994 that Iraq did have nuclear weapons ready for use. Also passed off as truth were Bush administration reports that President Hussein was supporting Al Qaeda units in Iraq and that Al Qaeda was responsible for the World Trade Center (WTC) attack, all of which was without foundation. Yet members of the Roaring Right Radio Network (RRRN) happily repeated these errors, notably Hannity and Combs and Fox News. Mr. Hannity obligingly told his audience that the weapons had been moved to Syria. He never offered a shred of evidence to support his statement. In addition to Fox News and other talk radio shows churn out masses of propaganda. Chief exponents of radio propaganda on behalf of the Bush administration are:

➤ Rush Limbaugh
➤ Matt Drudge

> Sean Hannity
> Bill O'Reilly
> Tucker Carlson
> Oliver North
> John Stossell
> Gordon Liddy
> Peggy Noona
> Larry King
> Michael Reagan
> Gordon Liddy
> Dick Morris
> William Bennett
> Michael Savage
> Joe Scarborough

Larry King is one of the best trained Tavistock puppets. When on the rare occasion he has an opponent of the Bush war on his show he will give them about 2 minutes to make their case, immediately followed by five pro-Bush "experts to rebut the daring dissenter."

Nearly all of the foregoing radio personalities have received instruction from the experts at Tavistock to a greater or lesser degree. When one studies their methodology, it bears a distinct resemblance to the methods of presentation perfected at Tavistock. The same can be seen in the television personalities, the "news anchors" and their message "news" that differs neither in content or style of delivery. Without exception they all bear the imprint of the Tavistock Institute.

The United States is in the grip of the greatest and sustained of mass mind control (brainwashing) and "conditioning" program and it is reflected at every level of our society. The masters of spin, deception, conniving, dissembling, half- truths and its twin brother, outright lies, have the American people by the throat.

Churchill, before he was "turned" declared in the House of Commons that the Bolsheviks "have seized Russia by the hair of its head." We make bold to say that "Tavistock has seized the head and the minds of the American people."

Unless there is a great awakening of Spirit of 1776 and the revival that took place among the generation that followed the Founding Fathers, the United States is doomed to collapse, even as the Greek and Ronan civilizations collapsed.

What is needed is the formation of our own "invisible army" of "shock troops" that will go into every village, every town, every city across the length and breadth of the United States, to deliver the counterpunch that will send the Tavistock troops into full retreat and ultimate defeat.

APPENDIX

THE GREAT DEPRESSION

Montagu Norman, then Governor of the Bank of England, and a close friend of the family of the Fabian Socialist, Beatrice Potter Webb, paid a surprise visit to the United States as a prelude to ushering in the Great Depression. As can be seen, this was a "contrived event" like the sinking of the Lusitania that brought the U.S. into WWI.

Events leading up to the Great World Depression of the 1930's

1928

Feb. 23—Montagu Norman visits M. Moreau, President of the Bank of France.

June 14—Herbert Hoover nominated for President by the Republican Party.

Aug. 18—Montagu Norman reelected President of the Bank of England.

Nov. 6—Herbert Hoover elected President of the U.S.A.

Nov. 17—Montagu Norman reelected Governor of the Bank of England.

1929

Jan. 1—The *New York Times* states, that a heavy flight of gold from the U.S.A. was expected in 1929.

Jan. 14—Eugene R. Black was reelected Governor of the Federal Reserve Bank of Atlanta, Georgia.

Jan. 26—Press reports indicate that forthcoming visit of Montagu Norman has no connection with the movement of gold from New York to London.

Jan. 30—Montagu Norman arrives in New York City; claims he is merely paying a courtesy visit to G.L. Harrison.

Jan. 31—Montagu Norman spends day with Federal Reserve Bank officials.

Feb. 4—Montagu Norman states no immediate change in the sterling or gold situation expected to arise from his visit. Congressman Loring M. Black, Jr., introduces a resolution asking the Federal Reserve Board, whether it had conferred with Montagu Norman at or about the time it had issued its credit warning.

Feb. 10—Rep. Black introduces a resolution asking President Coolidge and Secretary Mellon to clarify Norman's visit not as an official of the Bank of England

Feb. 12—Andrews says claim that Federal Reserve Bank has lost control of the money situation is an illusion and stated the Bank can regulate the market at will through action on rediscounts. His statement "triggered repeated charges that the Federal Reserve System has lost control of the economy. "

Feb. 19—Black's resolutions were defeated in the Banking and Currency Committee.

Feb. 26—The New York Times reports that many banks had

asked the Federal Advisory Council to cooperate in curbing loans for stock speculation.

Mar. 4—Herbert Hoover sworn in as President.

Mar. 12—Secretary of Treasury Mellon says he will not interfere with Board policy.

Mar. 21—Federal Reserve Bank of Chicago moves to reduce stock loans by 25 to 50% reduction in borrowing for speculation.

Apr. 1—National City Bank's April review of economy asks discount rate rise to 6% as way for curbing excessive stock speculation. A Rockefeller bank!

May 5—Kansas City Federal Reserve Bank raises rediscount rates to 5%.

May 14—Minneapolis Federal Reserve Bank raises rediscount rates to 5%.

May 19—The rise of rediscount rate to 5% is declared to be uniform; request for 6% rate by New York and Chicago denied.

May 23—Advisory Council recommends 6% rediscount rate.

Aug. 9—New York Federal Reserve Bank raised rate to 6%; it was called "adroit" measure.

Sep. 3—National City Bank (a Rockefeller-Standard Oil bank) in its monthly bulletin states the effect of the increase in the rediscount rate uncertain.

Oct. 29—Stock market crash ends post war prosperity; 16,000.000 shares, including unrestricted short selling, change hands.

By end of year decline in value of stocks reaches $15,000,000,000; by end of 1931 stock losses reached $50,000.000.000.

Nov.—New York Federal Reserve Bank reduces rediscount rate to 5%.

Nov. 11—Montagu Norman elected Governor of the Bank of England for eleventh term.

Nov. 15—Rediscount rate reduced to $4^{1/2}$%.

Throughout the early part of 1929 there were constant reports of shipments of gold to the United States to and from London, thus creating the impression, that the report of January 1 was accurate. With the stock market crash, however, the flight of gold from the U.S.A. commenced, in earnest.

Kurt Lewin

Kurt Lewin's (1890-1947) work had a profound impact on social psychology and experiential learning, group dynamics and action research. Lewin was born on September 9, 1890 in the village of Mogilno in Prussia (now part of Poland). He was one of four children in a middle class Jewish family (his father owned a small general store and a farm).

They moved to Berlin when he was fifteen and he was enrolled in the Gymnasium. In 1909 Kurt Lewin entered the University of Freiberg to study medicine. He then transferred to the University of Munich to study biology. Around this time he became in involved in the Socialist movement. His particular concerns appear to have been the combating of anti-Semitism and the democratization of German institutions.

His doctorate was received from the University of Berlin where he developed an interest in the philosophy of science and encountered Gestalt psychology. His PhD was awarded in 1916, but by then he was serving in the German army (he was injured in combat). In 1921 Kurt Lewin joined the Psychological Institute of the University of Berlin - where he gave seminars in both philosophy and psychology. He was starting to make a name for himself both in publishing and teaching. His work became known in America and he was invited to spend six months as a visiting professor at Stanford (1930). With the political position worsening considerably in Germany in 1933 he and his wife and daughter left for the United States.

Thereafter he became involved at the Tavistock Institute in various applied research initiatives linked to the war effort (the Second World War.) These included influencing the morale of the fighting troops and psychological warfare. He was always a strong Socialist. He founded the Center for Group Dynamics at MIT. He was also engaged in a program - the Commission of Community Interrelations in New York. The "T Groups" for which Lewin had become known emerged from this program which was directed toward solving religious and racial prejudices.

Lewin got funding for the Office of Naval Intelligence and worked closely in training its operatives. The National Training Laboratories was another of his mind-control mass brainwashing programs that played a profound role in the corporate world.

Niall Ferguson

Niall Ferguson is a history professor who taught at Cambridge and is now a tenured Oxford don. Those are the credential of a "court historian" whose main purpose is to protect the patriotic, political myths of his government.

Professor Fergusson, however has written an iconoclastic attack on one of the most venerable patriotic myths of the British, namely that of the First World War was a great and necessary war in which the British performed the noble act of intervening to protect Belgian neutrality, French freedom, and the empires of both the French and British from the military aggression of the hated Hun. Politicians like Lloyd George and Churchill argued that the war was not only necessary, but inevitable. In this they were ably assisted by the propaganda factory at Wellington House, "the house of lies" as Toynbee called it.

Ferguson asks and answers ten specific questions about the First World War, one of the most important being whether the war, with its total of ten million casualties, was worth it.

Not only does he answer in the negative, but concludes that the world war was not necessary or inevitable, but was instead the result of grossly erroneous decisions of British political leaders based on an improper perception of the "threat" to the British Empire posed by Germany. Ferguson regards it as "nothing less than the greatest error in modern history."

He goes further and puts most of the blame on the British because it was the British government that ultimately decided to turn the continental war into a world war.

He argues that the British had no legal obligation to protect Belgium or France and that the German naval build-up did not really menace the British.

British political leaders, Ferguson maintains, should have realized that the Germans were mostly fearful of being surrounded the growing Russian industrial and military might, as well as the large French army. He argues further, that the Kaiser would have honored his pledge to London, offered on the eve of the war, to guarantee French and Belgium territorial integrity in exchange for Britain's neutrality.

Ferguson concludes that "Britain's decision to intervene was the result of secret planning by her generals and diplomats, which dated back to 1905" and that it was based on a misreading of German intentions, "which were imagined to be Napoleonic in scale." Political calculations also played their part in bringing on war. Ferguson notes that Foreign Minister Edward Grey provided the leadership that put Britain on the bellicose path. Although a majority of the other ministers were hesitant. "In the end they agreed to support Grey, partly for fear of being turned out of office and letting in the Tories."

Such was the power of the lies and propaganda that flowed out of Wellington House, the forerunner of the Tavistock Institute of Human Relations.

The First World War continues to disturb the British psyche today, much as the Civil War still haunts Americans. British casualties in the war numbered 723,000 - more than twice the number suffered in World War II. The author writes: "The First World War remains the worst thing the people of my country have ever had to endure."

One of the most important costs of the war, which was prolonged by British and American participation, was the destruction of the Russian government.

Ferguson contends that in the absence of British intervention, the most likely result would have been a quick German victory with some territorial concessions in the east, but no Bolshevik Revolution.

There would have been no Lenin - and no Hitler either. "It was ultimately because of the war that both men were able to rise to establish barbaric despotisms which perpetrated still more mass murder."

Had the British stayed on the sidelines, Ferguson argues, their empire would still be strong and viable. He believes that the British could have easily coexisted with Germany, with which it had good relations before the war. But the British victory came at a price "far in excess of their gains" and "undid the first golden age of economic 'globalization.'" But ruthless anti-German propaganda turned those good relations into enmity and hatred.

World War I also led to a great loss of individual liberty. "Wartime Britain ... became by stages a kind of police state," Ferguson writes. Of course, liberty is always a casualty of war and the author compares the British situation with the draconian measures imposed in America by President Wilson.

The suppression of free speech in America "made a mockery of the Allied powers' claim to be fighting for freedom." What the Professor Fergusson did know was that Wilson had imposed the worst kind of restrictions of free speech. He even tried to get Senator La Follette arrested for opposing the war.

While Ferguson addressed mainly British audiences, it is relevant to Americans who tragically followed the brainwashed propaganda-dazed and nervously drunk British into both world wars at tremendous cost in freedom, the result of the centralization of power in the leviathan government in Washington, D.C.

There are many valuable lessons to be learned from this timely warning that the Tavistock Institute, successor to Wellington House, has shown just how easy it is to condition and mind-control large segments of population groups.

"The Great War:"

The Power of Propaganda

The fruits of the war that ordinary people of Britain, France, Germany, Belgium and Russia did not want: Killed in the prime of their lives:

Britain and Empire	2,998,671
France	1,357,800
Germany	2,037,700
Belgium	58,402

These are mainly deaths on the so-called "Western Front" and "Eastern Front" and do not include casualties sustained on other fronts by other nations. The cost in monetary terms was $180,000,000,000 in direct accounting and indirectly another $151,612,500,000.

The two WWI battles mentioned in this book:

Passchendaele. Began on July 31, 1917 the battle raged for three months. Casualties amounted to 400,000 men.

Verdun. Began February 21, 1916 and ended on June 7. 700.000 men killed.

Later Propaganda Efforts

Tavistock Institute has so perfected its techniques that recent expert opinion has it that 70% of all capital and human resources that the US government advertising/propaganda programs devotes to for strategic objectives, going to psychological operations, the propaganda which these psychological operations are comprised have become the single most significant part of what it means to be American and British.

The level of propaganda is now so, high, so all encompassing, that Social Scientist count on it to be the totality of American life, and as a result of sustained propaganda, life in these two countries has become a simulation. Tavistock predicts, as do philosophers and sociologists from Beaudrilliard to McLuhan, that this simulation will soon be substituted for reality.

The public perception of propaganda associates it with advertising and the kind of partisan propaganda disseminated by radio talk shows, or with a zealous radio preacher. Indeed these are all forms of propaganda, but for the most part they are recognized as such.

The advertiser is tries to instill his particular product or service on the minds of the audience. Political commentary does the very same thing and likewise religious programming is intended as much to motivate followers to take a particular course of action such as supporting the war or some country they ascribe as "biblical" we need to support at the exclusion of others) to change the spiritual orientation of non- committed listeners. Thus, they hope that audiences will be persuaded to embrace the ideas of the speakers or to follow their lead to support such and such an objective. Any "preaching" about the Middle East over American radio in particular soon reveals this objective.

Other types of communication in all forms of the media are far more intrusive such as deliberately slanted and or false, incomplete news reporting, presented as truth or objective fact. The reality is that it is naked propaganda disguised as news at which Tavistock graduates excel.

Forceful propaganda, first introduced by Bernays at Wellington House to forcefully persuade the unwilling population is by scientific repetition. World War I was a field day for Wellington House with thousands of reputations of "the Butcher of Berlin" etc.

In the latest Gulf war the people of the United States were not inclined to worry very much about an invasion by Saddam Hussein, but Powell, Rice, Cheney and a succession of "authorities" dinned it into the heads of the American people that Saddam Hussein might soon cause a "mushroom cloud" to appear over the United States, even though there was no truth in their claims.

The statement that "Saddam was a threat to his neighbors" stressed again and again — by government operatives and military leaders, who were soon joined by vast numbers of private organizations, political commentators, intellectuals, entertainers, and, of course, the news media carried the day even though based upon layers of lies.

Propaganda messages do differ although the core message is always the same and the sheer volume of warnings and the diversity of the sources involved served to confirm in people s minds that the threat is indeed very real. Slogans help listeners and readers of this propaganda material to visualize the "danger." orchestrated not so much to protect the country as to bring about active participation by raising the level of hysteria.

This was standard practice in use by Britain and the United States in all the wars in which they were combatants from 1900 up to the present time. The resulting climate of fear brought the desired effect; rapid expansion of military research and arms stockpiling and "pre-emptive strikes" in Serbia and Iraq.

Propaganda took a nasty fall during the Vietnam War when Americans actually saw the brutality of battle in their living rooms and the notion of a "defensive" war took a nosedive. The purveyors of the wars in Serbia and Iraq took good care not to allow the mistake to be repeated.

The effect of propaganda was so great that most Americans still believe that Vietnam was an "anti-communist" war. From the cold war generally — the Cuban missile crisis - Serbia propaganda helped hostilities to flourish and multiply.

The propaganda of the anti-communist era was tailor made by Tavistock and designed to facilitate the development of a global U.S. military expansion that has been going on since the Institute for Pacific Relations was established in the 1930s and upon which Mc McCarthy stumbled.

There are other type of insidious propaganda other types of propaganda are directed toward social behavior or group loyalties. We see it in the emergence of the decline in morals that has swept the world on a wave of well-directed propaganda of the type favored by H.V. Dicks, R Bion, Hadley Cantril and Edward Bernays, the Social Scientists who at one stage ran operations at Tavistock Their product, propaganda, is the illusion of truth fabricated by the whores of deception.

Bibliography

"Journey Into Madness;" Gordon Thomas

"MK. Ultra 90;" CIA

"American Journal of Psychiatry," Jan. 1956; Dr. Ewan Cameron.

Documents relating to activities of "The Society for the Investigation of Human Psychology." This was a front for CIA experiments into mind control.

"Ethics of Terror" Prof Abraham Kaplan.

"The Psychiatrist and Terror;" Prof. John Gun.

"The Techniques of Persuasion;" J.R. C. Brown.

"The Psychotic;" Understanding Madness; Andrew Crowcroft.

(When you understand "madness" it can be recreated in any subject.)

"The Battle for the Mind;" Private, Invicta Press.

"The Mind Possessed;" Private, Invicta Press.

"The Collected Works of Dr. Jose Delgado."

"The Experiments of Remote Mind Control" (ESB): Dr. Robert Heath.

Dr. Heath conducted successful experiments with ESB which proved that he could create memory lapses, cause sudden impulses (like random shootings), evoke fear, pleasure and hatred at his command.

"ESB Experiments;" Gottlieb.

Dr. Gottlieb said his experiments were leading to making a psycho-civilized person, and then, an entire psycho-civilized society, in which every human thought, emotion, sensation, desire is completely controlled by electrical stimulations of the brain.

Dr. Gottleib stated that he could stop a charging bull in its tracks; PROGRAM HUMANS TO KILL ON COMMAND.

Extensive documentation of experiments conducted by the CIA using ESB-the research under the control of Dr. Stephen Aldrich.

"The Collected Research Papers of Dr. Alan Cameron."

These were found with the huge collection of documents of mind control experiments packed away in 130 boxes, conducted by Dr. Gottleib and which he had not destroyed as ordered by the CIA.

"*The New York Times*, December 1974." An expose of CIA mind control experiments.

Apart from the above there is Dr. Coleman's own works, "Metaphysics, Mind Control, ELF Radiation and Weather Modifications" published in 1984, and updated 2005.

In this same work Dr. Coleman explains how mind control works and gives clear examples of it. He expanded on his earlier work with "Mind Control in the 20th Century," which explicitly details how mind control techniques have advanced.

A Dynamic Theory of Personality. Dr. Kurt Lewin

Time Perspective and Morale.

The Neurosis of War. W.R Bion. (Macmillan London 1943)

Experiences in Groups. (Lancet Nov. 27, 1943)

Leaderless Groups. (London 1940)

Experiences in Groups. (Bulletin of Messenger)

Catastrophic Change. (The British Psychoanalytical Soc.)

Elements of Psychoanalysis. London 1963

Borderline Personality Disorders. London

Force and Ideas. Walter Lippmann

Public Opinion. Walter Lippmann

Crystallizing Public Opinion. Edward Bernays

Propaganda. Edward Bernays

The Daily Mirror.

Alfred Harmsworth 1903/1904

The Sunday Mirror.

Alfred Harmsworth 1905/1915

Human Quality. Aurelio Peccei 1967

The Chasm Ahead. Aurelio Peccei

Wilhelm II, Emperor of Germany.

Memories of Lenin.

N. Krupskaya (London 1942)

The World Crisis. Winston Churchill

How We Advertised America. George Creel, New York 1920

Wilson, The New Freedom. Arthur S. Link 1956

The Aquarian Conspiracy. Marilyn Fergusson

Some Principles of Mass Persuasion. Dorwin Cartwright

Journal of Humanistic Psychology. John Rawlings Reese

Understanding Man's Behavior. Gordon Alport

Invasion from Mars. Hadley Cantrill

War of Worlds. H. G. Wells Terror by Radio.

The New York Times

Psychology of Science. Aldous Huxley

A Kings' Story. The Duke of Windsor

My Four Years in Germany. James W. Gerard

Under the Iron Heel. G. W. Stevens

The Technotronic Era. Zbigniew Brzezinski

Institute for Development and Management Publications. Ronald Lippert

When Action Research Becomes Cold War Methodology

The Science of Coercion. Renses Likert

Management Systems and Style. Mental Tensions. H.V. Dicks

The State of Psychiatry in British Psychiatry. H.V. Dicks

The Jungle. Upton Sinclair

Appeal to Reason The Money Changers.

Propaganda Techniques in the World War. Harold Lasswell

Imperial Twilight. Berita Harding

Innocence and Experience. Gregory Bateson

For God's Sake. Bateson and Margaret Meade

They Threw God Out Of the Garden. R.D. Laing

Steps to an Ecology of Mind. The Facts of Life.

On Our Way. Franklin D. Roosevelt

How Democracies Perish. Jean Francois Revel

Disraeli. Stanley Weintraub

Brute Force: Allied Strategy Tactics WWII. John Ellis

The Concentration Camps in South Africa. Napier Davitt

The Times History of the War in South Africa. Sampson Low 7 Vols.

The Organization's Man, Jorgen Schleiman 1965

Stalin and German Communism, Jorgen Schleiman 1948

Willi Munzenberg A Political Biography Babetta Gross 1974

Propaganda Technique in the World War Harold Lowell

The Propaganda Menace Frederick E. Lumley 1933

History of the Russian Communist Party Leonard Schapiro 1960

Neue Zurcher Zeitung December 21, 1957

The Bolshevik Rise to Power and the November Revolution, A.P. Kerensky 1935

Ten Days That Shook The World, John Reed 1919

Other titles

OMNIA VERITAS LTD PRESENTS:

ABORTION
GENOCIDE IN AMERICA

BY JOHN COLEMAN

I MAINTAIN THAT WHEN A WOMAN AGREES TO AN ABORTION IN A NON-LIFE THREATENING SITUATION, SHE HAS TAKEN LEAVE OF HER SENSES AND SHOULD BE ADJUDGED "TEMPORARILY INSANE."

ABORTION SHOULD BE EXPLAINED AS EUPHEMISM FOR "MURDER BY DECEPTION"

OMNIA VERITAS LTD PRESENTS:

THE CLUB OF ROME
THE THINK TANK OF THE NEW WORLD ORDER

BY JOHN COLEMAN

The many tragic and explosive events of the 20th century didn't happen by themselves, but were planned according to a well-established pattern...

Who were the planners and creators of these major events?

OMNIA VERITAS LTD PRESENTS:

DIPLOMACY BY DECEPTION
AN ACCOUNT OF THE TREASONOUS CONDUCT BY THE GOVERNMENTS OF BRITAIN AND THE UNITED STATES

BY JOHN COLEMAN

The story of the creation of the United Nations is a classic case of diplomacy by deception

ONE WORLD ORDER SOCIALIST DICTATORSHIP

BY JOHN COLEMAN

All these years, while our attention was focused on the evils of communism in Moscow, the socialists in Washington were busy stealing from America!

"The enemy in Washington is more to be feared than the enemy in Moscow."

WE FIGHT FOR OIL

BY JOHN COLEMAN

The story of the oil industry takes us into the twists and turns of "diplomacy".

The struggle to monopolize the resource coveted by all nations

BEYOND the CONSPIRACY
UNMASKING THE INVISIBLE WORLD GOVERNMENT

by John Coleman

All great historical events are planned in secret by men who surround themselves with total discretion.

Highly organized groups always have the advantage over citizens

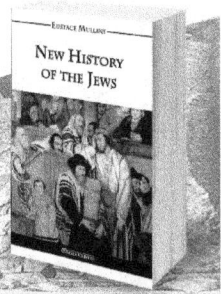

OMNIA VERITAS

Omnia Veritas Ltd presents:

NEW HISTORY OF THE JEWS

by

EUSTACE MULLINS

Throughout the history of civilization, one particular problem of mankind has remained constant.

Only one people bas irritated its host nations in every part of the civilized world

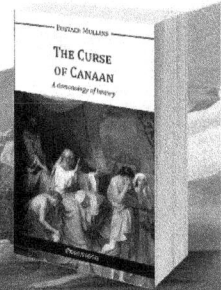

OMNIA VERITAS

Omnia Veritas Ltd presents:

THE CURSE OF CANAAN

A demonology of history

by

EUSTACE MULLINS

Liberalism, more popularly known as secular humanism, can be traced in an unbroken line all the way back to the Biblical "Curse of Canaan."

Humanism is the logical result of the demonology of history

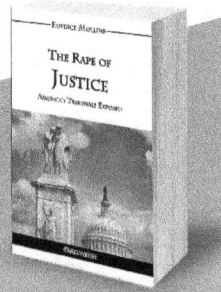

OMNIA VERITAS

Omnia Veritas Ltd presents:

THE RAPE OF JUSTICE

by

EUSTACE MULLINS

AMERICA'S TRIBUNALS EXPOSED

American should know just what is going on in our courts

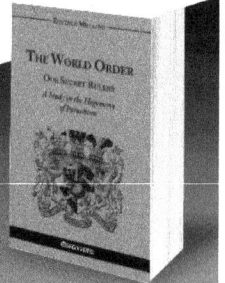

OMNIA VERITAS

It can be stated without fear of exaggeration that no book in the present century has been the object of so many commentaries in the world press...

Omnia Veritas Ltd presents:

The plot against the Church

by MAURICE PINAY

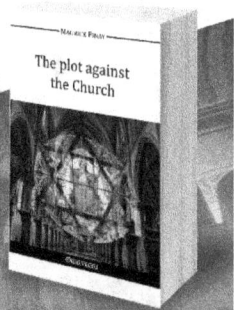

A magnificent and imposing compilation of documents and sources of undeniable importance and authenticity

OMNIA VERITAS OMNIA VERITAS LTD PRESENTS

THE DISPOSSESSED MAJORITY

THE TRAGIC AND HUMILIATING FATE OF THE AMERICAN MAJORITY

OMNIA VERITAS. OMNIA VERITAS LTD PRESENTS:

SOLZHENITSYN

The Jews Before the Revolution

"The purpose that guides me throughout this work on the life common the Russians and the Jews consists of looking for all the points necessary for a mutual understanding, all the possible voices which, once we get rid of the bitterness of the past, can lead us towards the future."

The Jewish people is at the same time an active and passive element of History

www.ingramcontent.com/pod-product-compliance
Lightning Source LLC
Chambersburg PA
CBHW070756270326
41927CB00010B/2162